MINISTRY OF THE WORD
-SEEDS OF FAITH-

MINISTRY OF THE WORD
–SEEDS OF FAITH–

Pastor Dr. James R. Boyd

MINISTRY OF THE WORD
-SEEDS OF FAITH-

Copyright © 2024 by Pastor Dr. James R. Boyd

All rights reserved. No part of this book may be used or reproduced in any manner whatsoever without written permission except in the case of brief quotations embodied in critical articles and reviews.

Author Pastor Dr. James R. Boyd's books may be purchased for educational, business, or sales promotional use. For more information, email jrboyd60@gmail.com

Scripture quotations taken from the New King James Version (NKJV) Copyright 1979, 1980, and 1982 by Thomas Nelson, Inc. Used by permission. All rights reserved.

Cover Design by: Pastor Dr. James R. Boyd & Owen Watson, Ph.D.

Editor: Owen Watson, Ph.D.

Library of Congress Cataloging-in-Publication Data

ISBN-978-1-957420-12-7

DEDICATION

This book is dedicated to my family. Not just those who share my DNA or bloodline, but those who are connected to me by the blood of Jesus Christ. This is for those who read the word of God and search for the application to their lives, and those who have an uncommon thirst to be in God's presence always.

CONTENTS

Introduction
No Fight Needed .... Day 1
Friends In High Places .... Day 2
Thank Him .... Day 3
In The Spirit .... Day 4
God's Favor .... Day 5
Best Guarantee .... Day 6
The Right Side .... Day 7
Spiritual Suicide .... Day 8
God Is Speaking .... Day 9
Are You A Divider .... Day 10
A Higher Hope .... Day 11
The Keeper .... Day 12
Wrong Focus .... Day 13
God Is Not Smiling .... Day 14
A Good Place .... Day 15
The Greatest Gift .... Day 16
God Changes Names .... Day 17
Truth In Prayer .... Day 18
We Are The Upright .... Day 19
The King Is Here .... Day 20
Willing To Live .... Day 21

Better Knowledge	Day 22
Further Trusting	Day 23
A Forever Possession	Day 24
The most precious gift	Day 25
His Goodness	Day 26
Blessed Children	Day 27
Love Them Instead	Day 28
Unbeatable God	Day 29
Tasty Fruit	Day 30
Sobering Thought	Day 31
God's Deal	Day 32
Faith Is The Key	Day 33
Ugly Temptation	Day 34
Tell It	Day 35
Faith Investment	Day 36
Treasure of Wisdom	Day 37
Lead By Light	Day 38
The Magnificent Seven	Day 39
Use Money Wisely	Day 40
Any Day Now	Day 41
Trusting In The Storm	Day 42
Too Heavy	Day 43
Enjoy God's Love	Day 44
Without Warning	Day 45
Sin's Temptation Costs	Day 46
Worthy Praise	Day 47
Hear The Word	Day 48

Eternal Joy	Day 49
Light of God's Love	Day 50
God Is Watching	Day 51
Treasure At Home	Day 52
Add To Your Faith	Day 53
Common Sense	Day 53
Be Free	Day 54
Rebuke Gently	Day 55
No Limits	Day 56
Speak Love	Day 57
Best Instruction	Day 58
What Questions Do	Day 59
You Have?	Day 59
Time To Get Serious	Day 60
Share The Wealth	Day 61
God's Greatest Creation	Day 62
No Limits	Day 63
Here They Come Again	Day 64
Secret Place	Day 65
Pray For The Family	Day 66
Have Faith In God	Day 67
Praise God Everybody	Day 68
No Bad Fruit	Day 69
A Better Way To Live	Day 70
Comfort In The Night	Day 71
Only His Love	Day 72
Wisdom Calls Constantly	Day 73

Righteous Workforce ....Day 74

Strong Faith..Day 75

Word Of Treasure...Day 76

Guard Your Anointing ....Day 77

More Than Enough ....Day 78

Chasing The Wind..Day 79

Follower ....Day 80

The Labor Is The Crown ....Day 81

Speak No Evil ....Day 82

A Wise Servant..Day 83

Time To Grow Up ....Day 84

Free Yourself...Day 85

Hear The Lord ....Day 86

All In ....Day 87

Be Humble ....Day 88

His Justice ....Day 89

He Knows..Day 90

A Wise King..Day 91

Praise Him...Day 92

Heart Of The Teacher..Day 93

Place Of Blessing..Day 94

Path To God ....Day 95

Quiet Truth..Day 96

The Lord Delivers ....Day 97

Internal Teacher..Day 98

Light Of Truth..Day 99

Growing Prudent...Day 100

Seek God's Face	Day 101
Seek Good Fruit	Day 102
Pride: A Toxic Jewel	Day 103
Just Abide	Day 104
Key To Freedom	Day 105
Watch Your Spirit	Day 106
No Anxiety	Day 107
Grace Is Good	Day 108
Approach Gently	Day 109
Jesus Prays	Day 110
Confidence Of God	Day 111
Overcoming Love	Day 112
Just Be There	Day 113
Prepare Your Praise	Day 114
With Me, Or Against Me?	Day 115
Teach Them Good	Day 116
Steps To Faith	Day 117
God's Treasure	Day 118
Godly Correction	Day 119
The Beauty Of Mercy	Day 120
Speak Peace	Day 121
See Yourself	Day 122
Practicing Ambassadors	Day 123
Get Holiness	Day 124
God Our Guide	Day 125
Follow The Maker	Day 126
The Best Way	Day 127

The Good Life	Day 128
A Better Use	Day 129
Please The King	Day 130
Sharing The Anointing	Day 131
Don't Miss It	Day 132
Get Up, Lazy Ones	Day 133
You Will See	Day 134
Open Your Gift	Day 135
Guard Wisdom	Day 136
Speak What Should Be Heard	Day 137
Failure Is Not An Option	Day 138
Love Choice	Day 139
A Glorious Answer	Day 140
No Other God	Day 141
Preach And Live	Day 142
Evil Is Not For You	Day 143
His Hands Work	Day 144
Simple Is Better	Day 145
Work Is Love	Day 146
Such Magnificence	Day 147
Power To Do It	Day 148
Strong Wisdom	Day 149
Willing Student	Day 150
Still Serving	Day 151
Guard Your Heart	Day 152
Fireproof Works	Day 153
Phony Faith Fails	Day 154

Half The Battle	Day 155
Wear It Well	Day 156
Avoid Scams	Day 157
Repent	Day 158
Listen To The Teacher	Day 159
Teachers Warn	Day 160
Cause Me	Day 161
More Than Blood	Day 162
Here I Am, Lord	Day 163
Be Exceedingly Glad	Day 164
Keep Your Bags Packed	Day 165
Draw Close To Jesus	Day 166
God On Your Side	Day 167
Check Your Heart	Day 168
Lazy Is Not For You	Day 169
If They Can Praise	Day 170
Share The Riches	Day 171
A Better Path	Day 172
Righteous Blessings	Day 173
Faithful Vigilance	Day 174
Short Life Or Long Life	Day 175
Lift Him Up!	Day 176
Manifesting Godly Men	Day 177
Wicked Is Not Good	Day 178
Change Direction	Day 179
Correct Them Right	Day 180
He Answers Your Call	Day 181

Sent To Labor	Day 182
What Do You Have	Day 183
A Righteous Throne	Day 184
No Time To Judge	Day 185
Just A Test	Day 186
Audience Of One	Day 187
Walk Through The Wilderness	Day 188
Gentle Discipline	Day 189
God Makes It Right	Day 190
Lend A Hand	Day 191
The Battle Within	Day 192
Dusty Return	Day 193
Good Seed	Day 194
Don't Lose Hope	Day 195
Thirsty For Living Water	Day 196
Stand, Don't Fall	Day 197
Know The Difference	Day 198
Speak It And Mean It	Day 199
The Highest Degree	Day 200
Banish The Darkness	Day 201
Speak His Word	Day 202
Contagious Love	Day 203
A Special Gift	Day 204
Trust His Timing	Day 205
Who Is Speaking?	Day 206
A Clear Path	Day 207
He Is God	Day 208

Know God	Day 209
Cut Off From God	Day 210
Wait And Pray	Day 211
Drink Deep	Day 212
Light Of Truth	Day 213
Be Washed	Day 214
Sharing Good News	Day 215
Path To Inner Peace	Day 216
"Gimme" Gets In The Way	Day 217
Good Fragrance	Day 218
Be Faithful	Day 219
Choose To Turn	Day 220
Time To Change	Day 221
See The Right	Day 222
A Joyful Song	Day 223
Not Like You	Day 224
Price Too High	Day 225
Real Worship	Day 226
Show Them The Way	Day 227
Take The Favor	Day 228
Faithfully Serving	Day 229
A Courteous Tradition	Day 230
Be Like Jesus	Day 231
Look To The Hills	Day 232
Family Reunion	Day 233
Chasing God's Riches	Day 234
Trusting Him	Day 235

Go Home	Day 236
Are You Ready Now?	Day 237
A Familiar Voice	Day 238
Better Way	Day 239
Shine In The Darkness	Day 240
Wise Choice	Day 241
He Is Here	Day 242
Wait For The Trumpet	Day 243
God's Ways	Day 244
Truth Disperses Lies	Day 245
Your First Disciple	Day 246
What You Need	Day 247
Guard Your Heart	Day 248
Soul Maintenance	Day 249
Time To Work	Day 250
Wash Up	Day 251
God Is Still Here	Day 252
Are You A Watchman?	Day 253
Seek Better	Day 254
Jesus Saves	Day 255
Settled	Day 256
Good Fear	Day 257
Let Your Angels Rest	Day 258
Choose The Promise	Day 259
Guard Your Mouth	Day 260
Raise A Praise	Day 261
Hard Work	Day 262

Smell The Roses Later	Day 263
Obedience Is Better	Day 264
Priceless Soul	Day 265
Choose The Shining Path	Day 266
Protected In My Work	Day 267
Glory Working	Day 268
Wise Use of Seed	Day 269
Blessed Wonder	Day 270
Good Treasure	Day 271
Say It Well	Day 272
Work In Progress	Day 273
Destined To Overcome	Day 274
Righteous Rise	Day 275
Light In Darkness	Day 276
Good Thoughts	Day 277
Hear Wisdom Cry	Day 278
Wonderful God	Day 279
As A Child	Day 280
Choose Wisdom	Day 281
Your Destiny	Day 282
Check Your Seal	Day 283
Get Good Counsel	Day 284
Through It All	Day 285
Untouchable	Day 286
Better Nutrition	Day 287
I Have Learned	Day 288
Heed His Direction	Day 289

Speak No Evil	Day 290
Right Faith	Day 291
Riches Await	Day 292
Battle Ready	Day 293
If You Will	Day 294
Unstoppable	Day 295
Let's Do It	Day 296
Believe Unto Righteousness	Day 297
A Sure Reward	Day 298
A Good Day To Trust	Day 299
The Right Path	Day 300
No Shame Here	Day 301
Let Love Conquer	Day 302
God Can Carry It	Day 303
Grow Up	Day 304
Room For Love	Day 305
A Need For Power	Day 306
Looks Like A Shepherd	Day 307
Shine Your Light	Day 308
Looking For Mercy	Day 309
Pruning Season Is Here	Day 310
Too Strong To Fight	Day 311
No Secret To God	Day 312
It Is Simple	Day 313
Listen To A Holy Tongue	Day 314
A Second Opinion	Day 315
Lift Him Higher	Day 316

Friend Or Foe	Day 317
Do You Know Him?	Day 318
Crown Of Trials	Day 319
Do Snakes Smile?	Day 320
Thank God	Day 321
A Worthy Question	Day 322
Wisdom Is The Way	Day 323
In The Sanctuary	Day 324
Do The Right Work	Day 325
No Fun In Sin	Day 326
Quiet Worship	Day 327
Serve The Body	Day 328
Different Is Good	Day 329
No Other God	Day 330
Living Anew	Day 331
Twists And Turns	Day 332
Peace, Be Still	Day 333
Strong Commandments	Day 334
Wise Counsel	Day 335
Choose His Teaching	Day 336
Secret Revealed	Day 337
Who's Celebrating?	Day 338
Cry Of Your Heart	Day 339
Walk In Worship	Day 340
Be Filled With God	Day 341
Precepts First	Day 342
Highest Wisdom	Day 343

Seek To Escape ....Day 344
The Day Awaits ....Day 345
You Are Enough ....Day 346
True Beauty ....Day 347
Sing Praises ....Day 348
Content With God ....Day 349
Worth The Climb ....Day 350
Protect The Foundations ....Day 351
Failing Each Other ....Day 352
The Ultimate Friend ....Day 353
Miracle Worker ....Day 354
Can You Hear Him? ....Day 355
Consider The Poor ....Day 356
Open The Gates ....Day 357
Go Deep ....Day 358
Listen Carefully ....Day 359
Love In Battle ....Day 360
What's Next? ....Day 361
Your Quiet Prayer ....Day 362
Graced With Gray ....Day 363
Push For Your Purpose ....Day 364
Wisdom Of Prayer ....Day 365
In Closing

INTRODUCTION

Acts 6:4 states, "But we will give ourselves continually to prayer and to the ministry of the word." With this declaration, the disciples outlined their task for the church they served. They would serve the people by providing to them the Word of God. As the deacons attended to the people's physical needs, disciples would attend to their spiritual needs. By giving (consistently and diligently saturating) themselves to prayer, they would hear from God, and be spiritually fed by God.

I pray that these devotional reflections will draw each reader closer to God through a deeper consideration of what God's Spirit is speaking to your spirit.

As you read these devotions, I pray that the Holy Spirit will stir up the gifts within you, that you may partner with other believers to bear fruit for God today.

In His Service,
Pastor James R. Boyd, ThD

DAY 1

NO FIGHT NEEDED

"But avoid foolish disputes, genealogies, contentions, and strivings about the law; for they are unprofitable and useless." –*Titus 3:9*

The spiritual war rages in the world, yet some of the most contentious battles are seen within the camp of Christians. We draw lines of battle based upon cultural and political preferences, with loose reference to scripture. How can we lead the world to Jesus when we seldom seek Him? A house divided by political disagreement will not truly unite against the sin that destroys. When our study of scripture is focused on finding those which prove that we are right – then in truth we are wrong. Avoid becoming a weapon for the enemy. Lift up the principles that edify. When you disagree on points that are not clear in scripture – concede gracefully. Be sure that the Holy Spirit will eventually bring clarity to understanding. This battle is not ours, but the Lord's. Avoid foolish disputes and contentions.

DAY 2

FRIENDS IN HIGH PLACES

"He who loves purity of heart and has grace on his lips, the king will be his friend." –*Proverbs 22:11*

Three Things

1. Purity of heart is to be loved
2. We speak grace to those who need
3. Kings seek those with character

We don't need to seek recognition and support from the world. When we follow the teachings of the Lord, He will elevate us in due time. But to receive honor from the outside, we must have good things on the inside. With purity of heart, we face life honestly, and truth becomes a prize possession. We can then speak from what is in our heart, and words of grace come easily. Such integrity is noticed by those in position of power. They will seek your wisdom and friendship. You cannot fake your way to higher levels, but true devotion to God will take you to the level where you are most effective. Your ability to serve, and humility while doing so, will bring you friends in high places.

DAY 3

THANK HIM

"Be anxious for nothing, but in everything by prayer and supplication, with thanksgiving, let your requests be made known to God; and the peace of God, which surpasses all understanding, will guard your hearts and minds through Christ Jesus." *–Philippians 4:6-7*

Three Things

1. Don't be anxious, no matter what faces you
2. Pray to God, He will hear you
3. Thanksgiving brings peace

This season may bring many things to invite concern. But I encourage a time of prayer, along with thanksgiving for what God has already done. Just rest beside the still waters for a time and enjoy the table He has prepared for you. His blessings are undeniable, and you never need to worry when He is with you. He is always with you. Shalom.

DAY 4

IN THE SPIRIT

"But the natural man does not receive the things of the Spirit of God, for they are foolishness to him; nor can he know them, because they are spiritually discerned. But he who is spiritual judges all things, yet he himself is rightly judged by no one." –*1 Corinthians 2:14-15*

Three Things

1. The natural man cannot receive spiritual things
2. Discernment is not a physical thing
3. Judgment is rightly received spiritually

He who is not born again lives in the flesh, and the natural consequence is death. This man cannot receive the things of the Spirit of God and cannot see what can only be spiritually discerned. That is only natural. But those born of the Spirit of God receive discernment by that Spirit. So, he can discern the things of God because he is connected to God. Such spiritual discernment allows for wisdom, knowledge, and true judgement to be applied to even natural circumstances. Yet those who are natural cannot judge what they cannot see with their physical eyes. So, they live on until the eyes of their understanding are enlightened.

DAY 5

GOD'S FAVOR

"Many seek the ruler's favor, but justice for man comes from the Lord." *–Proverbs 29:26*

Three Things

1. Many seek the ruler's favor
2. They look for justice in man
3. Justice for man comes from the Lord

Many hope that a ruler will be just, wise, and fair in deciding. So, they seek favor from that ruler, seeking a place of privilege for future consideration. But true justice can only come from the Lord, who sees all, knows all, and judges wisely. Scripture informs us that we should pray for our rulers and honor the fact that God has placed them in positions of authority. It is far better that we live humbly before God and keep our feet on the path of righteousness. That way leads to the favor of God and man. Seek the Lord. His favor is better.

DAY 6

BEST GUARANTEE

"The counsel of the Lord stands forever, the plans of His heart to all generations." –*Psalm 33:11*

God is not a temporary God. Anything that comes from the Lord will last throughout time. His counsel stands forever – hear His word. Do not add to it or deny it. God's counsel will come to pass. His plans, coming from His heart, will touch all generations. Scripture states that God knows the plans He has for His people, plans to give them a future and a hope. So, a foundation built on the counsel of God will not be shaken or denied. No better guarantee exists.

DAY 7

THE RIGHT SIDE

"Then Jesus said to them, "Children, have you any food? They answered Him, 'No.' And He said to them, 'Cast the net on the right side of the boat, and you will find some.' So, they cast, and now they were not able to draw it in because of the multitude of fish." –*John 21:5-6*

Somehow, Jesus appears at the right time, with the right questions. The word He speaks challenges us to take a different approach. Actions performed as the result of His direction will always lead to abundant blessings. His direction is still important today. Are you focusing your work on the right side of God's Word? Or have you cast your nets to draw in the greatest benefit for yourself? It is right to pray for, and care for others. It is right to live a life of faith, even when you leave the church building. It is right to treat others with respect and give grace to others when possible. That is the right side of the boat.

SPIRITUAL SUICIDE

"Whoever commits adultery with a woman lacks understanding; He who does so destroys his own soul." –*Proverbs 6:32*

Three Things

1. Adultery is destructive and sinful
2. Understanding comes too late
3. It destroys life and souls

Although God clearly forbids adultery, some practice it as a way of life. That leads to a toxic attitude that destroys all who are involved. A sense of entitlement leads to a loss of respect for God's Word, and the life of others. The lack of understanding regarding God's intent for marriage erodes future relationships. When one's conscience becomes seared, the soul begins to die. Distrust, anger and disrespect taint the life of habitual sinners. They have committed spiritual suicide.

But God has provided a way of escape for those trapped in this life; Resist, Repent, and allow God to Repair the damage. The Lord can bring life back to those who are dead in trespasses and sin. Accept Him.

DAY 9

GOD IS SPEAKING

"Then they cried out to the Lord in their trouble, and He saved them out of their distresses." *–Psalm 107:19*

Three Things

1. Trouble will cause you to cry out
2. Cry out to the Lord when trouble comes
3. He will save you

How often do we allow bad choices to get us into trouble? We can try to fix it ourselves, seek advice from friends, or even wait it out. But when trouble overwhelms, the best course of action is to cry out to the Lord. He will save you from your distresses when you are ready to listen. He has been speaking all along, but our pride can mute His voice in our hearing. When you cry out to Him, it clears the pride from your mind! Now you can hear Him. Scripture says that you will hear a voice whenever you go to the right or the left saying, "This is the way. Walk in it." (Isaiah 30:21). Now that your tears have washed the dust from your eyes, let's walk. God is speaking.

ARE YOU A DIVIDER

"Now I urge you, brethren, note those who cause divisions and offenses, contrary to the doctrine which you learned, and avoid them. For those who are such do not serve our Lord Jesus Christ, but their own belly, and by smooth words and flattering speech deceive the hearts of the simple." –*Romans 16:17-18*

In every organization, politics and selfishness demonstrates itself in divisions. In the Body of Christ, it should not be so. Yet the growth of denominations, splitting of churches, and the exit of Pastors from the ministry shows the depth of division. Jesus stated that they would know us by our love, one for another. Does He see that love in the church today? When we accept the gift of salvation, the Blood of Jesus removes our sin. Maybe we should apply that Blood to our attitude toward others, and in removing the pride that separates us from believers who are not "like us". Scripture reminds us to judge ourselves lest we be judged. What causes division in your circle? Is it you?

DAY 11

A HIGHER HOPE

"Hope deferred makes the heart sick, but when the desire comes, it is a tree of life." –*Proverbs 13:12*

Three Things

1. Life can make you defer hope
2. Such disappointment brings sickness
3. Renewed desire brings life

We dream of better things, and hoping for those things keeps us looking forward. When circumstances crush our dream, and we must defer our hope, some experience sickness. They struggle with anger, disappointment, and bitterness for years. Scripture informs us that Jesus comes to bring life more abundantly to those who choose His yoke. Casting your cares upon Him refreshes our hope and renews our life. As His Holy Spirit energizes our spirit, we desire to live for Him. How can despair exist in the light of His love? It will not. Seek Him, follow the path of holiness. Our hope is in Him. No higher hope exists. He is the highest hope.

DAY 12

THE KEEPER

"The Lord is your keeper; The Lord is your shade at your right hand. The sun shall not strike you by day, nor the moon by night." *–Psalm 121:5-6*

Three Things

1. The Lord is your keeper
2. He shades you by day
3. He protects you by night

God is your protector by day and night. Danger lurks on every side, yet God protected you when you were His enemy. As His child, you have work to do for Him. He loves you more than when you were unlovable. Faith is your protection, and the full armor of God is yours. Stop living in fear – that is not yours. Peace, love, and a sound mind is more than enough to deal with the enemy. God reminds us that He will keep us in perfect peace, whose mind is stayed on Him. If you are His child, you are safe under His wings. Learn to sleep in His arms. Tomorrow He will still be your keeper.

DAY 13

WRONG FOCUS

"Now John answered and said, 'Master, we saw someone casting out demons in Your name, and we forbade him because he does not follow with us.' But Jesus said to him, 'Do not forbid him, for he who is not against us is on our side.'" –*Luke 9:49-50*

If we are fighting the same enemy, why must we gather in the same field? The demons I see in my spiritual war may not register on your radar. Your secular job and training may sensitize you to that demon causing homelessness, while my skills gave me clarity about death and sickness. I will truly understand that you provide support to the troops fighting on another battlefront. I will not expect you to use my tactics. Confusion among Christians has led to harmful infighting, and a loss of effectiveness on our side. Does the enemy know that drawing a line along racial, pollical, or economic consideration can impact our battle readiness? He has shown that he does and uses that knowledge against us. Focus on God's Word, not men's opinion.

DAY 14

GOD IS NOT SMILING

"Bread gained by deceit is sweet to a man, but afterward his mouth will be filled with gravel." –*Proverbs 20:17*

Three Things

1. Some live by deceiving others
2. Ill-gotten gains may be sweet for a time
3. Revelation of lies brings judgement

There are entire industries built on deception and lies, that provide a good living for their workers. Scripture states that the wages of sin is death. So, one that deceives the innocent sins against God's standards of truth. Further, we reap what we sow. So, as we reap deceit to gain bread, we can count on "full-circle retribution" in due season. Yet, in spite of such knowledge, even some Christians are drawn to those who gleefully lie and deceive. They support their thievery by not condemning their actions. Be not deceived, God is not mocked. He also does not smile at sin.

A GOOD PLACE

"Know that the Lord, He is God; It is He who has made us, and not we ourselves; we are His people, and the sheep of His pasture."
–*Psalm 100:3*

Three Things

1. The Lord is God
2. He made us, not we ourselves
3. We are His people, the sheep of His pasture

When tempted by circumstances to question God, remember that He is God! Although we cannot understand why He performs the way He does, time will provide the wisdom of His way. Be comforted in the fact that we are His people, and the sheep of His pasture. That means that we are protected. No matter what. So don't run off to another field or listen to sheep who seem to have a carefree life without a Pastor. Remember the words of David; "The Lord is my Shepherd, I shall not want." Aren't you glad that the Lord is God? We are in a good place.

DAY 16

THE GREATEST GIFT

"Behold, the Virgin shall be with child, and bear a Son, and they shall call His name Immanuel; which is translated, 'God with us.'"
–*Matthew 1:23*

This is the season in which the world celebrates, drawn by the joy of love, and the promise of life. The miracle of a virgin birth brought forth the Son who would provide and fulfill. By living, He ushered in the joy of a Savior who would be with us, bringing the love, wisdom, and resources we did not know we needed. By dying, the Lamb of God took away the sin of man, giving a path to return to the Father who provides eternal life. There is no other way. When we give, we are following the example of a Father who gave His Son, and a Son who gave His life.

    Accept His gift of Salvation today. With that gift comes the Holy Spirit, who will live within your heart to guide you and comfort you. Your life can change today, if you just say "Yes" to the Greatest Gift.

DAY 17

GOD CHANGES NAMES

"The refining pot is for silver and the furnace for gold, and a man is valued by what others say of him." –*Proverbs 27:21*

Three Things

1. Certain conditions purify
2. Gold and silver need heat for processing
3. Men are revealed by reputation

The Lord surely tests man by His desires, and by his needs. Everything designed by God has a purpose, and we are not an exception. Silver and gold are refined by heat, with the intent of purifying them for greater worth. Man is tested by his circumstances, and his character revealed as his reputation grows. Scripture informs us that a good name is better than silver or gold. Many have begun their life's journey with reputations that were undesirable. With testing sent by God, and considerable obedience, they have forged a better reputation. Has God changed your name yet?

TRUTH IN PRAYER

"However, when He, the Spirit of truth, has come, He will guide you into all truth; for He will not speak on His own authority, but whatever He hears He will speak; and He will tell you things to come." *–John 16:13*

Wait for the truth. The Holy Spirit, the Spirit of truth, will bring comfort and guide into all truth. The world, with its' rushing, will convince you that fast decisions and hurried actions will place you ahead of the pack. Scripture reminds us that Jesus commanded His disciples to tarry (wait) until they were provided power from on high. For them, the Holy Spirit manifested as tongues of fire. For us, the Holy Spirit lives within us, and may manifest as wisdom, or the power of love shown to others. Our time of prayer allows us to remove ourselves from the world and seek guidance from God. Prayer is not a performance. It is a treasured time of sharing with God. That is truth!

DAY 19

WE ARE THE UPRIGHT

"For the upright will dwell in the land, and the blameless will remain in it." –*Proverbs 2:21*

Three Things

1. It is good to have a land to live in
2. The upright will dwell there
3. The blameless will remain in it

God has a plan for His people, where they will not need to wander or live in fear. That land, that contains every blessing, intended for abundant life, is not for the sinful. The upright will dwell in the land, teaching their children to fear the Lord and obey His Word. The blameless will remain in it, giving heed to the guidance of the Holy Spirit and walking in their integrity. This land exists, and the Lord seeks those with pure hearts to inhabit that land. God has provided us the land of blessings. We must now provide a people who seek God's face. We must become the upright who dwell here. If we are the upright, this is the land.

DAY 20

THE KING IS HERE

"Lift up your heads, O you gates! Lift up, you everlasting doors! And the King of glory shall come in." –*Psalm 24:9*

Three Things

1. We lift up the gates wide
2. We open the everlasting doors
3. The King of glory shall come in

We often prevent the King of glory from coming into our life. Sin, unbelief, pride, and other toxic things discourage Him from entering our life. But if we open the gates of our heart, and lift the door that guards our mind, He will come in. Scripture reminds us that He knocks at the door of our heart. If we open that door, He will come in and dine with us. The strongholds of our past are no match for the King of glory. One smile from Him, and the walls tumble down, as those of Jericho. Lift up your heads, O you people, and rejoice. The King is with us, and within us, by His Holy Spirit.

WILLING TO LIVE

"Who shall separate us from the love of Christ? Shall tribulation, or distress, or persecution, or famine, or nakedness, or peril, or sword? As it is written: 'For Your sake we are killed all day long; we are accounted as sheep for the slaughter.' Yet in all these things we are more than conquerors through Him who loved us." –*Romans 8:35-37*

Are you willing? We are confronted with a list of possible events that could separate us from the love of Christ. These are real situations that could be faced by any of us. Since Christ never takes His love away from us, we are in danger of taking our love from Him. Fear, pride, jealousy, disappointment, and many other weaknesses of the flesh can cause us to turn away from the love of Christ. Unless we fight. We fight a physical and spiritual war that requires us to be warriors for His name's sake. Through Him, we can be more than conquerors. Now that you see the potential enemies you face, I ask you again; "Are you willing to live for Christ?"

DAY 22

BETTER KNOWLEDGE

"Wise people store up knowledge, but the mouth of the foolish is near destruction." –*Proverbs 10:14*

Three Things

1. Knowledge is important
2. Wise people store up knowledge
3. Foolish ones talk their way into danger

How interesting the difference between those who know, and those who pretend to know. Wise people store up knowledge and speak when that knowledge is beneficial. Foolish ones know little, but their loud voices push others away, until they take charge as the leader. Unfortunately, ignorance will often lead to disaster. Willful ignorance is a form of pride. God does not bless pride. Scripture reminds us that the knowledge of the Holy One is understanding. Seek Him first, and His righteousness, and the Holy Spirit will guide you away from foolishness. Knowledge is the better way.

FURTHER TRUSTING

"Trust in the Lord, and do good; dwell in the land, and feed on His faithfulness." *–Psalm 37:3*

Three Things

1. Trust in the Lord and do good
2. Dwell consistently in the land
3. Feed on His faithfulness

When adversity arises, it is tempting to hide and complain. As warriors of God, we are called to trust in the Lord no matter how hard the road we travel. Trust that even this difficulty is part of His plan. But we must also continue to do good for others, and dwell consistently in the land we are sent. Stop gazing at another's green pasture and wishing you were there. Stand fast and work. Scripture reminds us to occupy until He returns. Defend your position with prayer and the Word of God. When your spirit gets weak, feed on His faithfulness. He has never failed you before and will not do so in the future. God's Word is truth. Trust in that.

A FOREVER POSSESSION

"Therefore let no one boast in men. For all things are yours: whether Paul or Apollos or Cephas, or the world or life or death, or things present or things to come – all are yours. And you are Christ's, and Christ is God's." *–1 Corinthians 3:21-23*

Don't let yourself be drawn into the worship of men. As a true child of God, you are given the same level of authority in the kingdom of God as even the most recognized people in society. Scripture reminds us that we have been given all things pertaining to life and godliness. Yet this knowledge is not given to pump pride into us. It must lead us to the holy structure – we are Christ's, and Christ is God's. With that awareness, we can truly do all things through Christ, who strengthens us. If you do not have Christ, you are outside of this promise. Fix that now. Accept Him, and He will be yours – forever.

THE MOST PRECIOUS GIFT

"A present is a precious stone in the eyes of its possessor; wherever he turns, he prospers." –*Proverbs 17:8*

Three Things

1. A present is a gift
2. It is precious to the possessor
3. Prosperity comes from that gift

One that is able to afford giving a present sees himself differently. He is not trying to make it but can now bless someone else. The present he holds becomes precious in his sight, and he looks forward to sharing that present. When one adopts an attitude of giving, it draws treasure to you. An open heart attracts others with a like mind. They give, you prosper. The more valuable the present, the greater the return. Somehow, those that give the most reap the greatest rewards. God gave us His greatest gift – His Son. Jesus gave His life. We add to the equation by sharing the gospel. We have the most precious gift to share: Truth of God's Word.

DAY 26

HIS GOODNESS

"For You have been a shelter for me, a strong tower from the enemy. I will abide in Your tabernacle forever; I will trust in the shelter of Your wings. Selah." *–Psalm 61:3-4*

Three Things

1. God is a shelter and strong tower
2. We can abide in His tabernacle
3. We can trust in the shelter of His wings

After the danger passes, in the lull following the storm, we can see that God has protected us. How often has the enemy surrounded us, with no way of escape, and God guided us to His strong tower? Trust in the Lord, and the shelter of His wings. There is peace in the tabernacle of the Lord. There you will find rest for your soul. Let us reason together. What has the world promised that compares to the goodness of the Lord? Taste and see that the Lord is good. Think about it.

DAY 27

BLESSED CHILDREN

"Now to Abraham and his seed were the promises made. He does not say, 'And to seeds' as of many, but as of one, 'And to your Seed,' who is Christ." –*Galatians 3:16*

You cannot step into another's house and take what does not belong to you. That would be theft. So, it is important that we recognize what belongs to us, versus what rightfully belongs to others. Scripture clearly designates the framework of each promise made. That is why we must "study to show ourselves approved", and not be carried away emotionally. Here is a truth to be considered, if the promises were made to Abraham's Seed (Jesus), don't we receive them through Christ? The answer is obvious. He has given us all things pertaining to life and godliness, scripture tells us. But we miss out when we miss Christ. Accept Him now and follow Him. Then you can receive every promise and blessing reserved for His children. Be truly blessed.

DAY 28

LOVE THEM INSTEAD

"Do not rejoice when your enemy falls, and do not let your hearts be glad, when he stumbles; lest the Lord see it, and it displeases Him, and He turn away His wrath from him." –*Proverbs 24:17-18*

Three Things

1. Do not rejoice at your enemy's trouble
2. That attitude does not please God
3. He could turn His wrath away

There is an old saying "God don't like ugly!" When you rejoice at the misfortune of others, even your enemy, God is not pleased. He might turn His wrath away from your enemy. It is never good to make God angry. Scripture states that we should treat our enemies with love, and even provide what they need. This pleases God and can make your enemies feel like you are heaping hot coals on their head. Love is always a better answer. So, when your enemy falls, don't laugh – love!

UNBEATABLE GOD

"Give us help from trouble, for the help of man is useless. Through God we will do valiantly, for it is He who shall tread down our enemies." –*Psalm 108:12-13*

Three Things

1. God's help is best
2. Through God we triumph
3. He treads down our enemies

In time of trouble, seek God. Men promise but cannot deliver. God's promises never fail. When your enemies oppose you, bringing their warriors of doubt, fear, and despair, call on the Lord. Through God, the darkness is defeated, and you will prosper. God is a present help in time of trouble. Scripture reminds us that we are more than conquerors through Christ Jesus. So, when you struggle against enemies that cannot be seen, call on Him who sees everything. He can never lose. He is unbeatable.

DAY 30

TASTY FRUIT

"But the fruit of the Spirit is love, joy, peace, longsuffering, kindness, goodness, faithfulness, gentleness, self-control. Against such there is no law." –*Galatians 5:22-23*

This is the fruit that can only grow in God's garden. Planted in the good seed of faith and obedience, tended by the Holy Spirit, aided by maturity. We seek this fruit in our life. Such fruit gives life and nurtures godliness. In the presence of those who seek the fruit of the Spirit, the presence of Jesus Christ reigns. Fellowship among the saints is sweet when this fruit hangs from the branches of humility. No tension, no rebellion, no law besides those given by Jesus. Love one another as Christ has loved you. If they are in need, share your fruit with them. The fruit of the Spirit fulfills every hunger. Taste and see!

DAY 31

SOBERING THOUGHT

"Give strong drink to him who is perishing, and wine to those who are bitter of heart. Let him drink and forget his poverty, and remember his misery no more." –*Proverbs 31:6-7*

Three Things

1. Dying people need strong drink
2. Bitter people need wine
3. Drinking brings forgetfulness

Alcohol in many forms provides an escape from life for many. The reality of death, or the bitterness of life can be comforted by the consumption of liquid spirits. Far better to face life's struggles with a clear mind and a healthy soul. Scripture reminds us that our body is the temple of the Holy Spirit. Keeping a temple clean and pure is difficult if you invite things in to defile it. We have the right to choose under God's grace. Let your choice reflect the honor you show toward your temple. Be sober, be vigilant! Your adversary, the devil, is prowling about seeking whom he may devour. That is a sobering thought.

DAY 32

GOD'S DEAL

"Why should the Gentiles say, "So where is their God?" But our God is in heaven; He does whatever He pleases." –*Psalm 115:2-3*

Three Things

1. Some ask where God is
2. The true God is in heaven
3. He does whatever He pleases

We hear that phrase at times: "Where is God when....?" Usually attached to a tragedy or personal loss. It is a question doubting God, His power, His love, or His intentions. This lack of faith is prompted by the little "gods" who promise to give everything but only destroy ultimately. Selfishness, lust, idolatry, money, fame can all become "gods" in our lives if allowed to reign. When we accept Christ, we become children of the God who lives in heaven but sends the Holy Spirit to love within us. How is that possible? He is God, and He does whatever He pleases. Give Him your heart, and He will give you the Kingdom. That is a good deal from a good God.

FAITH IS THE KEY

"Therefore, having been justified by faith, we have peace with God through our Lord Jesus Christ, through whom also we have access by faith into this grace in which we stand, and rejoice in hope of the glory of God." –*Romans 5:1-2*

Tribulation, wars, pestilence surround us in this world, but, yet we maintain our hope. We live in this world, but our soul stays fixed on the promise of the next. How can that be that we have peace with God? Through faith we have been saved. Not of works that we did, but through grace that came by the hand of Jesus Christ. Faith drew us to the truth of the cross, and by faith we live even now. Faith that leads to a living hope that one day we will see Him face to face. When we behold His glory, all questions will be answered, all doubt erased, all tears comforted, and all needs satisfied. Until then, we must continue sharing the good news of the Kingdom wherever we are. We have the key: it is faith.

DAY 34

UGLY TEMPTATION

"Immediately he went after her, as an ox goes to the slaughter, or as a fool to the correction of the stocks, till an arrow struck his liver. As a bird hastens to the snare, he did not know it would cost his life."
–*Proverbs 7:22-23*

Three Things

1. -We hasten to go after sin that tempts
2. Ignorance blinds us to danger
3. Death results from temptation

How beautiful is the temptation of sin, and how quickly we can be convinced to follow after it. But the dangers that kill are often not seen until too late. Satan enters with three traps: the lust of the flesh, the lust of the eyes, and the pride of life. His goal is to kill, steal, and destroy. Walk away from that which tempts the body or appeals to pride. Let your soul be guided by the Holy Spirit. If it is not of God, you don't need it. Sin may look good, but it turns ugly before it kills. Yield not unto temptation.

TELL IT

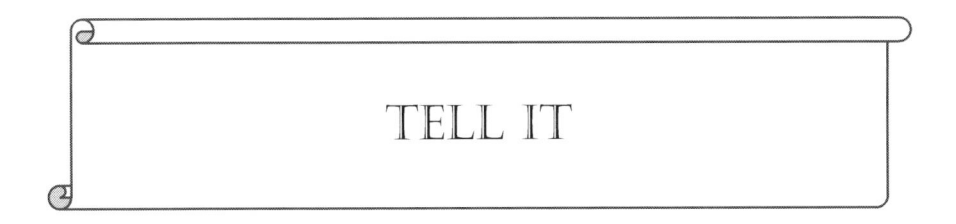

"Come and hear, all you who fear God, and I will declare what He has done for my soul." –*Psalm 66:16*

Three Things

1. I have a testimony to declare
2. Those who fear God need to hear
3. He has blessed my soul

Those who fear God should hear good things about God. Scripture states that the redeemed of the Lord should say so. When you share a testimony of God's grace, you speak truth. You tell of how God's favor enlightens your soul. Would this not encourage all to seek the Lord even stronger? When we gather as one in God's house, shouldn't we hear confirmation that He still answers prayer? He is the same yesterday, today, and forever. But some will not believe until they hear what God is doing right now. The world can be dirty, dark, and disappointing. Shine a light on God's goodness. Stand up and tell it!

DAY 36

FAITH INVESTMENT

"Blessed be the God and Father of our Lord Jesus Christ, who according to His abundant mercy has begotten us again to a living hope through the resurrection of Jesus Christ from the dead, to an inheritance incorruptible and undefiled and that does not fade away, reserved in heaven for you." *–1 Peter 1:3-4*

His mercy led to His sacrifice, leading to our reward through faith. If we have hope, we are living for the glory to come. No hope, no life. We are crucified with Christ, scripture reminds us, and we will be raised as joint heirs with Him. We receive grace when we have faith. And our obedience leads to righteousness. Have you considered the benefits available to Children of God? Your faith investment pays eternal rewards. Nothing else compares. Live and hope, believe and declare. The Lord is God, and He values good investments.

TREASURE OF WISDOM

"A scoffer seeks wisdom and does not find it, but knowledge is easy to him who understands." –*Proverbs 14:6*

Three Things

1. Some scoff at things they don't understand
2. Those do not find the wisdom they seek
3. Those who understand find knowledge everywhere

Some laugh and scoff at things they do not understand. They seek wisdom but fail to recognize it. When others are blessed with knowledge that leads to wisdom, scoffers laugh or grow bitter. Nothing is serious to a scoffer. But those who seek to understand see beyond the obvious. They dig deep into the knowledge that unfolds before them. Like seasoned treasure hunters, they see value in the knowledge they gain. While scoffers declare that "knowledge puffs up", the wise understand that we serve a God of infinite knowledge. That God gives good gifts to His children; teaching, wisdom, knowledge, and understanding. Move the scoffers aside, wisdom is close by.

DAY 38

LEAD BY LIGHT

"Lead me, O Lord, in Your righteousness because of my enemies; make Your way straight before my face." *–Psalm 5:8*

Three Things

1. Enemies can confuse the path
2. The Lord can lead in righteousness
3. He will make His way straight

More enemies bring more confusion. They can guide you into crooked paths, leading to destruction. But the Lord will lead you into His righteousness, making the way straight and undeniable. Beware of those who claim to know a "better way" to happiness. If their path leads away from Jesus, it will lead to destruction. This world is famous for short cuts and easy living. Avoid it and follow the Lord. Even if He leads you through the valley of the shadow of death, you know He is with you. Crooked paths lead to crooked places. Stay on the straight and narrow path. The Lord will light the way.

THE MAGNIFICENT SEVEN

"Therefore, brethren, seek out from among you seven men of good reputation, full of the Holy Spirit and wisdom, whom we may appoint over this business." –*Acts 6:3*

The business of the church, family and even secular dealings, must be guided by integrity, faith and diligence. We cannot separate who we are in the world, from who we present in a "religious" situation. Reputation results from consistent actions. Before God, you cannot "fake it till you make it". The world may accept a self-declaration for a while, but God requires total obedience. His requirement is simple, but impossible to accomplish without the Holy Spirit. "To do justly, to love mercy, and to walk humbly with your God." If you do that consistently, you may qualify to be one of the magnificent seven.

DAY 40

USE MONEY WISELY

"The rich rules over the poor, and the borrower is servant to the lender." *–Proverbs 22:7*

Three Things

1. Lack of money creates difficulty
2. Rich people rule over the poor
3. Borrowers are servants to the lender

In the world's economy, money determines the position in which you live. Without money, one is subject to the rule of the rich. Even if one can borrow money, the lend can then make one a servant. Money is a necessary tool for living on earth. A wise person will assess the gifts and skills they have and determine what worth those skills have. By increasing their skills through education and experience, it is possible to add great wealth to your household. Scripture reminds us that the love of money is the root of all kinds of evil. So don't love it. Just learn how to use it wisely.

DAY 41

ANY DAY NOW

"Return, O Lord! How long? And have compassion on Your servants. Oh, satisfy us early with Your mercy, that we may rejoice and be glad all our days!" –*Psalm 90:13-14*

Three Things

1. When will the Lord return?
2. Satisfy Your servants with mercy and compassion
3. We will rejoice and be glad all our days

Even as we wait for the promised return of the Lord, we serve Him by serving His children. We pray for compassion and mercy, as we cannot live without His grace. Scripture reminds us that in His presence is fullness of joy. So, we yearn to see His face, that our souls may rejoice. Yet, He has told us to occupy until He comes. So, we work, in sure obedience, knowing that He will return. Any day, any hour, any minute now. Don't let your lamp of hope go out. It lights a path to your heart. He is on His way.

DAY 42

TRUSTING IN THE STORM

"In Him you also trusted after you heard the word of truth, the gospel of your salvation: in whom also, having believed, you were sealed with the Holy Spirit of promise." *–Ephesians 1:13*

Hearing the word of truth led to your believing the gospel of Jesus Christ unto salvation. You trusted Him, with a joy that was intoxicating. Maturity in the faith taught you that you were sealed with the Holy Spirit of Promise the day of your salvation. That Holy Spirit dwells within you even now. But now you hear of wars, and rumors of wars. Pestilence, earthquakes, and disaster dominate the news. Love is scarce, and hatred threatens to divide even the church. Where do you go? Who do you trust? Run to the Word. Scripture tells us that if we call to Him, He will answer, and show us great and mighty things. Trust Him. He alone has the plan. As for the storms – enter the shelter of His love. Storms always pass.

TOO HEAVY

"He who covers his sins will not prosper, but whoever confesses and forsakes them will have mercy." –*Proverbs 28:13*

Three Things

1. Some cover their sins for shame
2. Confession must also be forsaking
3. God will have mercy

Some go to great lengths to cover their sins, either for shame or for deceit. Scripture reminds us that we may be sure that our sin will find us out. But if we confess our sins, God is faithful and just to forgive us our sin. The mercy of God results in removal of all sin. But we must accept the fact that we are sinners in order to confess and forsake that sin. Only God can touch our heart to act on removing our sin. Without that, we duck and cover, denying the truth. No prosperity can thrive in such a darkness. Sin is too heavy a burden to carry. Bring it to Jesus. His burden is light.

ENJOY GOD'S LOVE

"Lord, what is man, that You take knowledge of him? Or the son of man, that You are mindful of him?" –*Psalm 144:3*

Three Things

1. The Lord knows about man
2. God knows and is mindful of everything
3. Only He can answer these questions

Philosophers have sought answers to the question of man's purpose and identity. Most have fallen short in that quest. Only the Lord, who formed man from the dust of the earth, knows why man is so important to Him. The Son of man, as Jesus often referred to himself as, played a crucial part in bringing man back to fellowship with God. Scripture states that we were reconciled to God through the death of His Son. John 3:16 gives the foundation of God's love for us, but not the reason for that love. Man is the crowning creation of God. But our true worth appears when, through salvation, we become children of God. When we get to heaven, we can ask – "Lord, why did You love us so?" Until then, let's enjoy it.

WITHOUT WARNING

"But concerning the times and the seasons, brethren, you have no need that I should write to you. For you yourselves know perfectly that the day of the Lord so comes as a thief in the night."
–*1 Thessalonians 5:1-2*

The signs are all around us, growing more unmistakable each day. Jesus is coming back soon. Man is ignoring this truth, and the toxic lifestyle of many proves that. Yet even more have learned to tolerate that which before would be intolerable. Scripture reminds us that in these times, we must become serious in our prayers. We are also to be watchful as we pray, knowing that our redemption grows nearer. As the world revolves in chaos, we must stand firm on the truth. Nehemiah built the walls of Jerusalem with his sword on his side. He was ready for any situation. There will be no memorandum before Jesus returns. Just be ready.

DAY 46

SIN'S TEMPTATION COSTS

"At times she was outside, at times in the open square, lurking at every corner." –*Proverbs 7:12*

Three Things

1. Sin's temptation is everywhere
2. It changes according to times
3. It lurks at every corner

Sin has no shame. It makes itself available everywhere. Where it is found depends upon the time, and the opportunity. Simply put, sin lurks at every corner. Scripture reminds us that our adversary, the devil, roams about seeking whom he may devour. Be warned that the hunt continues. Your protection lies in the presence of the Good Shepherd. Do not succumb to the temptations you see outside of His field. When He calls, return to your place of safety. Scripture is clear: the wages of sin is death. Too high a price to pay for a romp in another's pasture.

WORTHY PRAISE

"I will praise You forever, because You have done it; and in the presence of Your saints I will wait on Your name, for it is good."
–*Psalm 52:9*

Three Things

1. God has done what no one else could do
2. I will praise Him in the assembly
3. His name is good and worthy

Scripture states that we overcome by the Blood of the Lamb, and the Word of our testimony. The Lord has done for us what no one else could do: He gave us eternal life. For that, I will praise Him forever along with the saints who love Him and worship His name. So many do not share this joy, because they have not yet heard the true gospel. If you are one of His saints, it is time to share this truth.

If you know, you must go! The harvest is waiting.

HEAR THE WORD

"But Simon answered, and said to Him, 'Master, we have toiled all night and caught nothing; nevertheless, at Your Word I will let down the net.' And when they had done this, they caught a great number of fish, and their net was breaking." –*Luke 5:5-6*

Life is filled with toil and even disappointment. It becomes more so when you know what to do and are diligent to perform the work. In those times, it is good to know that a Word from Jesus can turn that situation into great return. He understands the frustrations of life and knows where you should apply your gifts. After all, He provided both your gifts and the rewards. Yes, we should work. Scripture reveals that even God works. There is much to accomplish, and prayer is a part of that work. You will find that wisdom will join your team when you are obedient. Listen to His Word.

ETERNAL JOY

"Even in laughter, the heart may sorrow, and the end of mirth may be grief." *–Proverbs 14:13*

Three Things

1. We may laugh for many reasons
2. Sorrow may underline the laughter
3. When the laughter ends, comes grief

I have seen it at many homegoing celebrations; remembering the joyful time enjoyed with the departed loved one. The laughter as everyone remembers the good times of the past. Then the sober thought that the loved one has passed on, bringing a strong sense of grief. Both are good feelings, joy of knowing love, and grief from the absence of a loved one. Scripture reminds us that weeping may endure for a night, but joy comes in the morning. The medicine of love later heals temporarily, but the comfort from faith in the Lord is for eternity. We will all leave this earth eventually. Make sure your journey leads you to heaven, and the joy of salvation, the only eternal joy.

DAY 50

LIGHT OF GOD'S LOVE

"Why are you cast down, O my soul? And why are you disquieted within me? Hope in God, for I shall yet praise Him for the help of His countenance." –*Psalm 42:5*

Three Things

1. Our soul can be cast down
2. We can feel disquieted
3. But God can bring hope and help

Life can darken your soul, making you feel disquieted. The answer to such darkness is to hope in God, and to rely on the help of His countenance. When things all seem overwhelming, we must encourage ourselves in the Lord. Light dispels darkness, so the light of God's countenance removes the darkness of doubt. How can you refuse to praise a God who wants to flood your life with the light of His love? Ask yourself – is it worth living a life without God's light? Don't cast down your soul, cast down your doubt. Live in His light.

GOD IS WATCHING

"For we walk by faith, not by sight." *–2 Corinthians 5:7*

Each day reminds us that we are human – weak, confused and often guided by emotion. Considering the reality, it is amazing that we make it through each day. Here is another reality; God loves us. John 3:16 confirms that His love resulted in the greatest sacrifice the world has ever known. So here we are, suspended between the knowledge that we are favored children of God, and the hard realities of life! Which do we consider? BOTH! While we live on this earth, we perform the work required to live. Simultaneously, we protect our faith in God, believing that His plan for us is just ahead. Keep the faith, and let it guide our walk. We are moving through the valley of the shadow of death. Keep walking! Finally, don't get discouraged by the things you see. Watch and pray but be anxious for nothing. God sees your walk.

DAY 52

TREASURE AT HOME

"There is desirable treasure, and oil in the dwelling of the wise, but a foolish man squanders it." –*Proverbs 21:20*

Three Things

1. Good things can exist in your dwelling
2. Wise people store treasure and oil there
3. Foolish men squander it all

A comfortable dwelling requires more than furniture and food. It must be filled with safety, love, and hope for tomorrow. Surrounded by loved ones, the wise share the love of Jesus with each other, and all that enter the house. The treasure of love, and the oil of gladness so abundantly shared through the Holy Spirit, makes such a dwelling a joyful home. But scripture reminds us that the foolish tears down their home, despising and squandering the treasure contained within. Do not covet the life of those who seem to be wealthy. Invite Jesus into your home and live in truly abundant treasure.

DAY 53

ADD TO YOUR FAITH COMMON SENSE

"How precious is Your lovingkindness, O God! Therefore, the children of men put their trust under the shadow of Your wings."
–Psalm 36:7

Three Things

1. God's lovingkindness is precious
2. Children of men can trust Him
3. They exist under the shadow of His wings

When we consider the goodness of the Lord, we find that His lovingkindness is ever before us. His grace is sufficient for every need. Those who know put their trust in the Lord, believing that they are protected under the shadow of His wings. Scripture warns us not to test the Lord our God. So, avoid foolish actions just to show how blessed you are. Some cliffs are too high to chance a fall. Better to stay in God's favor by walking in His path of obedience. God has forgiven your sins, if you have accepted salvation through Christ. But if you do things that lead to injury, it will take time to heal. Common sense is a wonderful thing. Add it to your faith.

DAY 54

BE FREE

"Therefore, if the Son makes you free, you shall be free indeed."
–*John 8:36*

Today we hear a lot about freedom. But it is mostly freedom to do what we want to do. That freedom changes as our desires change. Jesus seeks a freedom for us, not for Himself. He promises freedom from sin, and all the negative symptoms that accompanies sin. He brings life abundant, but we cannot access it if we are chained to sin. Our adversary, the devil prefers that we never enter such an abundant life. So, he disrupts our mind, and clouds our perception. That is no way to live. Demanding freedom for your right to be bound to sin seems illogical. Free your mind, and your body will follow. Seek Jesus. His way leads to eternal freedom. When He frees you, the chains are shattered. Be free.

DAY 55

REBUKE GENTLY

"He who rebukes a man will find more favor afterward than he who flatters with the tongue." *–Proverbs 28:23*

Three Things

1. Sometimes rebukes are needed
2. Those corrected will appreciate it
3. Flattery may increase bad behavior

Some behavior is not pleasing to God. When we know that someone is demonstrating inappropriate behavior or attitudes, it is good for us to gently correct them. It may be that they are angry, distracted, or not aware of their impact through their behavior. Scripture informs us that faithful are the wounds of a friend. Better that your friend endures the paper cut of your correction, than the cutting off of their influence. It may sting, but they will appreciate it later. Those who flatter in the case of bad behavior often seek the demise of the person they flatter. Speak the truth in love and help those in need. Constant rebuke of others is a sign of pain in the rebuker. Rebuke gently.

DAY 56

NO LIMITS

"For I know that the Lord is great, and our Lord is above all gods. Whatever the Lord pleases He does, in heaven and in earth, in the seas and in all deep places." –*Psalm 135:5-6*

Three Things

1. The Lord is great and above all
2. He does what He pleases
3. He has no limits

We exist on the earth created by the Lord. He is great and cannot be compared to any god. He is above all things on the earth, above the earth, and under the earth. He does whatever He pleases because He is God. Scripture states that beside Him, there is no other. We can only know that the Lord is great if we have truly experienced the grace and favor that can only come from Him. In Him we love, and move, and have our being. We exist because of Him who holds all things together with His mighty hand. A God with no limits.

SPEAK LOVE

"Let no corrupt word proceed out of your mouth, but what is good for necessary edification, that it may impart grace to the hearers."
–Ephesians 4:29

God spoke words that created the world in which we live. His was a word of creation. Jesus spoke words of healing, grace and comfort to draw men back to a right relationship with God.

When we speak corrupt (rotten, worthless) words, it diminishes our ability to bring truth to the conversation. Credibility is hard won, but easily lost. As Cristians, we represent the principles taught by Christ. Those who hear us expect to be edified, or even corrected with love. We have been saved by His grace and travel the road of righteousness. It is necessary that our walk match our talk. Spiritual maturity includes growing up in our speech. If you would not speak to Jesus with those words, don't speak like that to others! Speak love.

DAY 58

BEST INSTRUCTION

"Take firm hold of instruction, do not let go; keep her, for she is your life." –*Proverbs 4:13*

Three Things

1. We learn by instruction
2. Remember what you have learned
3. Process of learning impacts your life

There are some who refuse instruction. It is not the case that they cannot learn, but that they will not learn. The process of learning prepares you for success in the future. Those who refuse to learn will find difficulty in their life. Pay attention to instruction. Discover how you learn best and hold strongly to that knowledge. Exercise the skill of lifelong learning. It will keep your mind active, and your spirit fresh. Jesus addressed the topic of instruction in Matthew 11:29 by stating, "Take My yoke upon you and learn from Me, for I am gentle and lowly in heart, and you will find rest for your souls". No better instructor than Jesus. Pay attention.

WHAT QUESTIONS DO YOU HAVE?

"O Lord, how great are Your works! Your thoughts are very deep. A senseless man does not know, nor does a fool understand this."
–Psalm 92:5-6

Three Things

1. The Lord's Words are great
2. He has deep thoughts
3. Senseless people don't know this

God engineered the heaven and the earth with wisdom and intent. Nothing happened by accident or circumstances. He thought deeply about the plans He set for us and included a plan for salvation leading to eternal life. Some trip their way through life, believing any popular notion that will allow for carefree and senseless living. They reject both personal responsibility and the truth of God. Consider, as you smell the roses, who created both those roses, and the dirt from which they grow. God knew that you would one day wonder what makes the flowers grow. He alone has the answers. What questions do you have?

TIME TO GET SERIOUS

"For this reason, the gospel was preached also to those who are dead, that they might be judged according to men in the flesh, but live according to God in the Spirit. But the end of all things is at hand; therefore, be serious and watchful in your prayers." *–1 Peter 4:6-7*

While we were dead in trespasses and sins, God yet loved us. He made certain that we could hear the gospel message that would bring us to eternal life with Him. So now we live with the assurance that our judgment will be under the atonement of the Blood of Jesus Christ. The warning is sounded; we are in the last days. Many have not taken the consequences of sin seriously. Perhaps because we have not delivered the truth seriously. The harvest is plentiful, the need is great. The time is now. Watch and pray as though someone's life depends upon it! This is serious.

SHARE THE WEALTH

"The generous soul will be made rich, and he who waters will also be watered himself." –*Proverbs 11:25*

Three Things

1. Generous people become rich
2. Watering others is good
3. You reap what you sow

The one who is generous with the blessings given by God will be made rich. Scripture reveals that God makes rich and adds no sorrow to it. When you water another with your own wisdom, support, or love, you will find that someone will water you. In that way, all of God's harvest grows. It is easy to understand: you reap what you sow. It is not limited to money. The gifts entrusted to you by God is infinitely more valuable than money. When you share those gifts, the worth just increases. You cannot expend love when you serve a God of love. Share, don't spend.

DAY 62

GOD'S GREATEST CREATION

"Those who go down to the sea in ships, who do business on great waters, they see the works of the Lord, and His wonders in the deep."
–Psalm 107:23-24

Three Things

1. Some do business on ships and great waters
2. They see the works of the Lord
3. They see His wonders in the deep

You cannot truly experience the great works of the Lord sitting on your couch. He has created great waters, deep seas, vast expanses of desert and jungles. Majestic mountains and plains. All able to take your breath away and remind you that He is God. The world exists outside of your house, away from the restriction of your classroom, apart from the security of your church. Take some time to see the creation of God, both close to your neighborhood, and in other countries. While you contemplate the creation of earth, appreciate the greatest creation – man. There is where you will see God's masterpiece. Think about it.

NO LIMITS

"For with God nothing will be impossible." *–Luke 1:37*

"How can this be?" Far too many times in our lives we question both the promises and the presence of God. Spiritual maturity brings us to the realization that He has already provided to us all things pertaining to life and godliness. Yet at certain times, He gives us more than we expect, in startling ways. The greatest miracle is His gift of eternal life, freely given to those of us who do not deserve it. And He continues to love us in spite of our deliberate rejection of His way. God knew you before you were placed in the womb. He planned a wonderful life for you, and even prepared for times you would fall. That is love. The most dangerous words for a Christian to say is – "I do not believe!" Believe in the miracles that God works. After all, you are one of them. No limits for God!

DAY 64

HERE THEY COME AGAIN

"The words of a talebearer are like tasty trifles, and they go down into the inmost body." –*Proverbs 18:8*

Three Things

1. Gossipers offer many words
2. Words that are tasty and useless
3. Words that can damage your spirit

You can almost see on their face that they have the latest gossip to share. Somehow, they know if you are as hungry for their toxic news as they are to share it. Don't be deceived by their friendly manner, their message is one of death. They are being used by the adversary to kill, steal and destroy. One translation of this scripture states that the words of a talebearer "are as wounds". They are designed to cut the person who hears it, or the person spoken of. That is not the behavior God expects from believers. If words do not edify, and bring another close to the Lord, it is best not to indulge in it.

DAY 65

SECRET PLACE

"You shall hide them in the secret place of Your presence, from the plots of man; You shall keep them secretly in a pavilion from the strife of tongues." –*Psalm 31:20*

Three Things

1. God can hide us in secret places
2. A place where no plots of man can reach us
3. Safe even from the strife of tongues

How we yearn to be in a place of safety and peace. God has that for us. Where His presence is hidden and secure. A secret place where the pavilion of His protection prevents even the plots of men to penetrate. Where the enemy dares not intrude, and we are safe even from the strife of tongues. Think not that we must travel far or live long to find this secret place. The Lord bids us to come away to Him, and He will give us rest. Beside the still waters are the green pastures prepared for us. If you seek Him, you will find Him. In the secret place of your soul.

DAY 66

PRAY FOR THE FAMILY

"For this reason we also, since the day we heard it, do not cease to pray for you, and to ask that you may be filled with the knowledge of His will in all wisdom and spiritual understanding." –*Colossians 1:9*

Not only should we pray for the Pastors and individual churches, but also for all churches and ministries in the region. Satan enjoys division, and sows confusion wherever he can. If we focus on the fact that we are the Body of Christ, we can embrace the task of praying for each other. Beginning with ourselves, we must seek to be filled with the knowledge of His will. That will bring the wisdom and spiritual understanding that leads to life abundance. Families thrive when they support and honor each other. That same consideration can apply to churches located in the same region. Pray for one another. We are family.

DAY 67

HAVE FAITH IN GOD

"Confidence in an unfaithful man in time of trouble is like a bad tooth and a foot out of joint." *–Proverbs 25:19*

Three Things

1. Do not rely on unfaithful men
2. Trouble reveals what we are made of
3. Pressure on bad body parts hurts

Scripture states that an unfaithful man is unsteady in all his ways. When trouble comes, those with no faith will run to safety, leaving us to live through the trouble on our own. That hurts, especially if we had confidence in that person. The truth is, many will experience the pain of trusting in people we later find to be with you only when times are good, or they receive what they want from you. That is a painful truth. When that time comes, remember the words of Jesus, "Father, forgive them, for they know not what they do." Smile and continue living. God loves you. Have faith in God.

DAY 68

PRAISE GOD EVERYBODY

"Let the peoples praise You, O God; let all the peoples praise You. Then the earth shall yield her increase; God, our own God, shall bless us." –*Psalm 67:5-6*

Three Things

1. Let all the peoples praise God
2. The earth shall yield her increase
3. God is our own God, and shall bless us

We praise God because He is God. All people who claim Him as our God, know that He alone is worthy of all praise. In praise, the earth shall yield her increase. Even in the face of resistance and adversity, we continue to praise Him. After all, we walk by faith, not by sight. Our praise is not limited to singing, or exuberant noise. We should praise God with our daily work. The joy in our heart drives the excellence of our commitment. When the world praises the gifts that God has given to you, they are praising God for that gift. Let all the people praise Him.

NO BAD FRUIT

"You will know them by their fruits. Do men gather grapes from thorn bushes, or figs from thistles? Even so, every good tree bears good fruit, but a bad tree bears bad fruit. A good tree cannot bear bad fruit, nor can a bad tree bear good fruit." –*Matthews 7:16-18*

What is in you will come out, no matter how much work is done to cover the defects. The produce (fruit) speaks of itself. When the soul is good, the person will focus on and work toward good. There are some who have learned to copy good speech and behavior, yet their soul (mind, will, and emotions) are intent on bearing bad fruit. Scripture notes that these are wolves in sheep's clothing. Your best defense is to accept the gift of salvation through Jesus Christ. The Holy Spirit will then reside within you, and discernment will reveal truth to you. Popular opinion will lead some to ignore this truth. They will end up stepping in rotten fruit, or maybe even producing their own. Be transformed and bear good fruit.

A BETTER WAY TO LIVE

"Whose ways are crooked, and who are devious in their paths."
–Proverbs 2:15

Three Things

1. Some should not be followed
2. Those whose ways are crooked
3. Those who walk devious paths

You know who they are. Everybody knows. Scam artists, thieves, workers of iniquity. In some circles, they are admired and followed. But that is not so for you, Child of God. Scripture advises you to walk in your integrity and avoid those who are devious in their ways. This world may reward those who injure the innocent, but God judges with a higher standard. Scripture notes that in the last days, many will be deceived. Don't believe that darkness is a good way to prosper. Walk in the light, as He is in the light. Stay on the straight and narrow path. It is a better way to live.

COMFORT IN THE NIGHT

"When I remember You on my bed, I meditate on You in the night watches. Because You have been my help, therefore in the shadow of Your wings I will rejoice." –*Psalm 63:6-7*

Three Things

1. I remember God on my bed
2. Meditate on God's help
3. Rejoice in His protection

At the end of a difficult day, before laying down to sleep, it is good to meditate on how good God has been this day. Reflection on His protection should bring rejoicing. If not for the goodness of the Lord, what tragedy could have come? Don't take God's grace for granted. A grateful heart is much appreciated. It leads to a real humility in our daily life. You really did not deserve His grace and mercy. The realization of that fact gives room for you to show more grace to others. And when you give grace, you please God. That should comfort you even more when you lay down to sleep.

ONLY HIS LOVE

"No one has seen God at any time. If we love one another, God abides in us, and His love has been perfected in us. By this we know that we abide in Him, and He in us, because He has given us of His Spirit."
–1 John 4:12-13

Our strength comes from love. We are strengthened by God's love and strengthen each other by the love we share. How encouraging to realize that we abide in Him, as we are perfected by His love that abides in us. It is not by might, nor by power, scripture states, but by His Spirit, says the Lord. So, I ask you today, Children of God, how are you honoring that love? Love flowing from the Spirit is not to be held captive but must flow freely. If He truly resides in you, that love will be there. Forget the power, seek the Love.

WISDOM CALLS CONSTANTLY

"She has sent out her maidens, she cries out from the highest places of the city." *–Proverbs 9:3*

Three Things

1. Wisdom has maidens (servants)
2. She cries out to those who hear
3. She is found in the highest places

Wisdom does not work alone. Anything that helps you acquire wisdom works for her. Those mistakes you made along the way were teachers that helped you. Those experiences that seemed to just be useless were teachers also. Wisdom is found at the highest level of every establishment. She is not silent. But in a world intent on itself, her voice often becomes clear when mistakes happen. So, one will learn from it, and gain wisdom. Since your road is long, and the ascent to the top is steep, listen for the voice of wisdom. Wisdom never stops talking.

DAY 74

RIGHTEOUS WORKFORCE

"I have been young, and now am old; yet I have not seen the righteous forsaken, nor His descendants begging bread." –*Psalm 37:25*

Three Things

1. Long life reveals much
2. God will not forsake the righteous
3. His descendants are not beggars

Life has many twists and turns. The longer we exist, the more things we see. But the promises of God to the righteous result in a place of distinction. He will not forsake the righteous. Their faith keeps them close to God. Further, their character drives them to work hard to provide. As their children grow, they see the unspoken message that is spoken in scripture – "he that will not work should not eat." His descendants are not beggars. So, the work continues for those who are righteous. The harvest is plentiful, but the workers are few. God provides for His people. We work hard to represent Him. As He works, so do we.

DAY 75

STRONG FAITH

"But without faith it is impossible to please Him, for he who comes to God must believe that He is, and that He is a rewarder of those who diligently seek Him." *–Hebrews 11:6*

Faith is not for the weak. It requires a knowing within that is almost illogical. We please God by coming to Him, knowing that He is. Is what? He is everything that we need. And He rewards those who diligently seek Him. Where do we seek Him? First, within ourselves. Scripture advises us to be still and know that He is God. Another scripture declares that faith comes by hearing, and by the Word of God. Stop chasing faith. Be still, hear the Word of God, and know that God is all you need. When you finally come to Him as a child, trusting and believing, God will be pleased. Be strong in the faith.

DAY 76

WORD OF TREASURE

"He who heeds the word wisely will find good, and whoever trusts in the Lord, happy is he." –*Proverbs 16:20*

Three Things

1. Heed the wisdom in the Word
2. You will find good there
3. Trust in the Lord and be happy

God's Word is not given as a vain exercise. If we heed His Word, and wisely follow the truth of it, we will find good. Scripture states that the Lord has given us all things pertaining to life and godliness. It is in His Word. But to receive those blessings, we must activate our faith. Trusting in Him leads up to a true reward. We find treasure that cannot be destroyed or stolen. What happiness we experience living for the Lord. Don't let the enemy deceive you to walk away from God's blessings. His Word is the treasure you seek. A limitless treasure.

GUARD YOUR ANOINTING

"He permitted no one to do them wrong; yes, He rebuked kings for their sakes, saying, "Do not touch My anointed ones, and do My prophets no harm." –*Psalm 105:14-15*

Three Things

1. God protects His own, who are doing His work
2. He rebukes those in authority
3. He sets forth stern warnings

Those who are in service to the Lord have a special assignment, and God's protection. Scripture notes that the steps of a righteous man are ordered by the Lord. There is a way that is to be followed. In that path, even those in authority are rebuked for trespasses against You. The message goes forth regarding the righteous: touch them not. Some use this to push their way into areas for which they are not called and reap the results of their disobedience. Walk in humility. If God sends you, serve with honor. Pride can remove your anointing. Guard it.

MORE THAN ENOUGH

"Now to Him who is able to do exceedingly abundantly above all that we ask or think, according to the power that works in us."
–*Ephesians 3:20*

We go to Him because first of all, "He is." The existence of God who created all things, and is everywhere we need Him to be, is our foundation of faith. We compound that with the assurance that "He is able." No doubt regarding that fact: He has never failed. He loves us. That love is seen daily, as He places His Holy Spirit within us, as a seal of His promise. That Holy Spirit is the power that moves us to our destiny as we serve God wholeheartedly. We are in the presence of a God who answers prayers before we ask, and He knows the intentions of our heart. What more could you ask for? No matter, it is already there. More than enough.

CHASING THE WIND

"Will you set your eyes on that which is not? For riches certainly make themselves wings; they fly away like an eagle toward heaven."
–*Proverbs 23:5*

Three Things

1. Wealth is a concept that cannot be seen
2. When you chase riches, they fly away
3. Far above your reach on earth

Some spend their lives chasing wealth, thinking it can be acquired by an act of willpower. Scheme after scheme proves to be fruitless, as they discover that speaking words must be followed by actual work. Scripture reminds us that God makes one rich and adds no sorrow to it. In that blessing, it comes to one who possesses humility and the fear of the Lord. If your greed and pride has convinced you that you deserve riches, consider that God resists the proud and gives grace to the humble. When you seek God's heart, blessings will chase you down. And you will have the wisdom to manage God's wealth.

DAY 80

FOLLOWER

"My soul follows close behind You; Your right hand upholds me."
–Psalm 63:8

Three Things

1. Trusting sheep follow their Shepherd
2. My soul follows close behind the Lord
3. His right hand upholds me

More than ever, we need to follow the Good Shepherd. The One who loves us enough to give His life for us. Who protects us from all danger and lifts us up with a strong right hand. I have seen Him through His Word, so my will, mind, and emotions follow close behind Him daily. Never too far away that I cannot hear His voice. I am one of the sheep of His pasture. I claim that gladly, knowing that the Lord leads me to green pastures. There is no better place than in the shadow of His wings. There is room enough for you. Come to the foot of the cross. Follow me as I follow Him. Be a follower.

DAY 81

THE LABOR IS THE CROWN

"Therefore, my beloved and longed-for brethren, my joy and crown, so stand fast in the Lord, beloved." –*Philippians 4:1*

This multi-level blessing and encouragement I share with Paul as I extend it to you. To brethren near and far away – stand strong. The world is not a friendly place to those who live by righteousness and faith. But Jesus warned that the world will hate us, because it hated Him first. We press on to share the good news with those who have not heard, and to instruct those who believe wrongly. We wield the weapons that cannot be defeated: truth and love. Our purpose is God-given, and our abilities are God-granted. As we use our talents to guide many to the truth of salvation through Christ Jesus, we shall one day receive a crown of righteousness. We labor for souls, not rewards.

DAY 82

SPEAK NO EVIL

"Do not malign a servant to his master, lest he curse you, and you be found guilty." –*Proverbs 30:10*

Three Things

1. Do not speak evil of a servant to his master
2. We are all servants of God
3. God could rightly accuse us of speaking evil

When we become servants of God, there is a danger that others may speak evil of us. Division by denomination makes it easier for us to talk about "them." In such conditions, our words may not be filled with love and grace. Sadly, because we disagree with the form of a Preacher, we might discount his message to others. Seek the heart of a fellow servant of God. If they don't know something, share your truth. Help each other grow in faith. This is not a competition for recognition. God sees us all. Speak no evil.

A WISE SERVANT

"Who knows the power of Your anger? For as the fear of You, so is Your wrath. So teach us to number our days, that we may gain a heart of wisdom." –*Psalm 90:11-12*

Three Things

1. Your anger is powerful
2. Our fear should reflect Your wrath
3. Teach us to regard our days, and gain a heart of wisdom

God's anger is powerful. Our fear of God should remember His wrath. Teach us to number our days, to reflect on the life we have lived. As we remember the goodness of God, and contemplate on His power, we gain a heart of wisdom. Too often we are confident in our own level of power. Scripture reminds us that power belongs to God. He gives a measure of wisdom and power to accomplish work for Him. So, when you have finished speaking His Word, and fighting His enemies: Bow. You are still just a servant.

DAY 84

TIME TO GROW UP

"…that we should no longer be children, tossed to and fro and carried about with every wind of doctrine, by the trickery of men, in the cunning craftiness of deceitful plotting, but, speaking the truth in love, may grow up in all things into Him who is the head – Christ."
–*Ephesians 4:14-15*

Following the crowd may comfort a need for safety but may open the doors to deception and forms of Christian superstition. If Jesus did not endorse it, and the real Apostles did not practice it, do not accept it. Scripture warns us to test the spirits to see if they are of God. When you search the scriptures, the truth becomes obvious. Then you must make a choice – follow God or follow man. Joshua made it clear when he declared, "As for me and my house, we will serve the Lord." Truth has the potential to separate, and some are offended by the truth. So let me say this gently but clearly – it is time to grow up.

FREE YOURSELF

"So do this, my son, and deliver yourself; for you have come into the hand of your friend: Go and humble yourself; plead with your friend." –*Proverbs 6:3*

Three Things

1. Your attitude and behavior can change responses from others
2. Approach your friend as a friend
3. Humble yourself to get forgiveness

Some situations can destroy you and your relationship with others. If your bad decisions have placed you in a bad situation, move quickly to resolve it. Go to your friend, humble yourself, and ask for forgiveness. Scripture reminds us that God resists the proud but gives grace to the humble! Those who need forgiveness are more ready to forgive. Do not remain in the bondage of pride. Humility can break many chains. Even those formed by your own mistakes. Free yourself.

HEAR THE LORD

"I will hear what God the Lord will speak, for He will speak peace to His people and to His saints; but let them not turn back to folly."
–Psalm 85:8

Three Things

1. Hear what God speaks
2. He speaks peace
3. But don't return to folly

When God speaks, it is wise to listen. He speaks peace to His people and to His saints. We need such peace to live in this world today, to do our work opposing the enemy. When God speaks peace, there is peace, surpassing all understanding. Scripture states that some are foolish by returning to their sin as a dog returns to his vomit. God is a forgiving God but will not always strive with man. Repent from foolishness and stay on the path of righteousness. That is what God speaks. Can you hear Him?

ALL IN

"For none of us lives to himself, and no one dies to himself. For if we live, we live to the Lord; and if we die, we die to the Lord. Therefore, whether we live or die, we are the Lord's." –*Romans 14:7-8*

In all that we do, we indeed serve at the pleasure of the King of kings. He paid the price for us, that we may live for Him. Our lives reflect our faith. If we believe that we have an assignment to make disciples, we use our gifts to demonstrate the glory of the Lord in our lives. No need to flood others with our religious zeal. The Holy Spirit, who resides within us can teach us the way to reach the lost. We see them every day. On the street, at work, even at home. When you seek righteousness, and walk with integrity, they will see the difference. We no longer live for ourselves, we live for the Lord. Be all in, or not at all. He knows who you serve.

DAY 88

BE HUMBLE

"Poverty and shame will come to him who disdains correction, but he who regards a rebuke will be honored." –*Proverbs 13:18*

Three Things

1. We all will receive correction
2. How we respond affects results
3. Better to learn and change behavior

From childhood, we depend on our parents to train and correct us, that we may learn the right way to live and behave. As Children of God, He corrects us as we work for His glory. But some are rebellious, refusing correction from any source. The result is societal rejection, and increased punishment (to include poverty and shame). The wiser ones hear the rebuke, consider better behavior, and change their actions. Such change leads to honor that keeps them on the path of righteousness. Being unique is a characteristic we all share. It does not relieve us of our responsibility to be humble. God does give grace to the humble. And that is good for us all.

HIS JUSTICE

"The Lord executes righteousness and justice for all who are oppressed." *–Psalm 103:6*

Three Things

1. The Lord is Judge over all things
2. He executes righteousness and justice
3. He stands for all who are oppressed

Such an unfair world we live in. No one seems to know what is right, and evil seems to devour the innocent. No champions stand to defend them, and each one is focused on their own problems. The eyes of the Lord are not closed, and His strong right arm is ready to set it all in righteousness. His mercy gives time for repentance, even as His hand holds back the tide of evil. Take heart, all who are oppressed. The Lord Himself executes righteousness and justice for you. His time is always perfect, and His grace is indeed sufficient. Pray for your enemies. His justice is coming soon.

HE KNOWS

"For we do not have a High Priest who cannot sympathize with our weaknesses, but was in all points tempted as we are, yet without sin. Let us therefore come boldly to the throne of grace, that we may obtain mercy and grace to help in time of need." –*Hebrews 4:15-16*

He knows. He is not ignorant to the difficulties of life, and the impossible choices it brings. We don't have to explain anything to Him. We just need to obey the Word He speaks. We can come boldly to the throne of grace, bringing our petitions and sorrows. What better place to go than to a High Priest who is also our Lord and Savior? A contrite heart is the only sacrifice He seeks. One day, He will dry every tear, as we dwell with Him eternally in heaven. But until that day, spend time in prayer, assured that He knows.

DAY 91

A WISE KING

"Mercy and truth preserve the king, and by lovingkindness he upholds his throne." –*Proverbs 20:28*

Three Things

1. Kings are known by their rule
2. Mercy and truth preserve the king
3. Lovingkindness upholds his throne

A king is known by the way he rules. A brutal king will be overthrown, and he will not be preserved. One that rules with mercy and truth is to be honored, and lovingkindness will uphold his throne. More than authority, a good king leads with love. He cares for those who have selected him as king. As he loves his people, they love him in return. The King of kings loved His people so much that He died for us. Scripture says that His kingdom will never end. The Only Wise King.

DAY 92

PRAISE HIM

"Let all those who seek You rejoice and be glad in You; let such as love Your salvation say continually, "The Lord be magnified."
–*Psalm 40:16*

Three Things

1. Those who seek You should rejoice
2. Some love Your salvation
3. They should magnify the Lord

We must seek the Lord while He may be found. Having found salvation in Him, we must rejoice that it is so. When we have realized the gift of love received, let us love Him even more. Lift your voices continually and magnify the Lord. Proclaim the good news to all that are downtrodden. The Lord saves. Mercy and peace are found in the way of His righteousness. So, His love shall enlighten our hearts. Lift your voice in praise!

HEART OF THE TEACHER

"But evil men and imposters will grow worse and worse, deceiving and being deceived. But you must continue in the thing which you have learned and been assured of, knowing from whom you have learned them." *–2 Timothy 3:13-14*

These times are filled with deception and half-truths, with some people set on taking advantage of the gullible. Scripture tells us that a great falling away (apostasy) will occur, as many walk away from the truth. We are seeing much of that now. Continuing in the truth of scripture is more critical now than ever before. But knowing from whom you have learned your understanding of scripture is also very important. Follow and learn from those who build your understanding with true knowledge. Emotion can cloud the mind, leading to deception. Who is teaching you, and what is their purpose? Know the heart of the teacher.

DAY 94

PLACE OF BLESSING

"Like a bird that wanders from its nest is a man who wanders from his place." *–Proverbs 27:8*

Three Things

1. Everything has a place
2. Wandering serves no purpose
3. God has you there purposefully

Birds build nests for safety, stability, and to nurture their young. To wander away from their nests is to abandon their responsibility before their purpose is fulfilled. Men are placed in accordance with God's purpose for each man. To wander away from that place is to reject God's purpose for positioning you there. Scripture states that all things work together for good, in accordance with God's purpose. Remain in your place until God moves you to the next place of blessing. And yes, they are all places of God's blessing.

PATH TO GOD

"For the Lord knows the way of the righteous, but the way of the ungodly shall perish." –*Psalm 1:6*

Three Things

1. We choose the way of our life
2. God knows the way of the righteous
3. The way of the ungodly is death

We can choose the way we go, but the consequences of our choice will affect our eternity. The way of righteousness is one that leads to God. He knows that way because He walks with us in righteousness. The way of ungodliness takes us away from God. It is marked by pride, and every evil way. Scripture reminds us that the wages of sin is death. When we walk in ungodliness, we reap the wages of that sin. Read the signs and turn away from ungodliness. Seek the way or righteousness and walk the path that God knows. It leads to Him because He built it.

QUIET TRUTH

"And being found in appearance as a man, He humbled Himself and became obedient to the point of death, even the death of the cross."
–*Philippians 2:8*

Your circumstances do not relieve you of your responsibility. The work must be completed. Higher levels of authority often require deeper levels of sacrifice. Scripture reveals that he who would be the greatest in God's kingdom must be the greater servant. That takes both humility and obedience. In a world marked by selfish ambition, it takes great strength to be humble. If you are in the Body of Christ, the example Christ set is undeniable. We serve to show His love. We are obedient to His commandments. And while we go into the world to make disciples, our focus is not on ourselves! We can declare truth quietly. Quiet truth is still truth.

THE LORD DELIVERS

The righteous cry out and the Lord hears, and delivers them out of all their troubles." –*Psalm 34:17*

Three Things

1. In trouble, we all cry out for help
2. The righteous cry out, and the Lord comes
3. He delivers them out of all troubles

Trouble comes unexpectedly and threatens to overwhelm us. It is natural for us to cry out for help when we are in danger. When the righteous cry out, the Lord hears their cries. His love will not let them remain in that condition. So, He delivers them out of all their troubles. The righteous walk on the path of righteousness, so many of their troubles arise from serving the Lord. Scripture reminds us to count it all joy when we encounter such trials. But no matter how dire the circumstances, don't despair. The Lord will deliver. He always does.

DAY 98

INTERNAL TEACHER

"But the anointing which you have received from Him abides in you, and you do not need that anyone teach you; but as the same anointing teaches you concerning all things, and is true, and is not a lie, and just as it has taught you, you will abide in Him." *–1 John 2:27*

The Holy Spirit anoints and teaches, reminding us of those things that Jesus spoke. The truth of the Word lies in His Word. When we seek "additional" confirmation from other sources, we are in danger of deception. Ask the Holy Spirit for guidance regarding the Word of God. Scripture reminds us that He has given us all things pertaining to life and godliness. When we seek to rightly divide the Word of truth, the anointing of the Holy Spirit is invaluable. When you are preparing to pass that Algebra test, study helps.

DAY 99

LIGHT OF TRUTH

"My son, do not walk in the way with them, keep your foot from their path." *–Proverbs 1:15*

Three Things

1. Some walk the wrong path in life
2. Do not be persuaded to walk with them
3. Avoid the path they travel

There have always been people who exist in a darker environment, who survive by wrongful means. Society has enamored some of that behavior, admiring their actions. But you, believer, are called to a higher level of responsibility. Do not be persuaded to walk with them or desire their things. Scripture reminds us that the Lord makes us rich and adds no sorrow to it. Better to toil for honest rewards than to face shame later for dishonest gain. Do not follow those whose behavior reflects a devious or evil character. They will reveal the truth eventually. Avoid the path they travel. Ask the Lord for wisdom. He will shine the light of truth.

GROWING PRUDENT

"The simple inherit folly, but the prudent are crowned with knowledge." –*Proverbs 14:18*

Three Things

1. A person can be foolish or prudent
2. Environment can contribute much
3. We grow foolishness or knowledge

Scripture reminds us to train a child in the way he should go, but foolish parents providing a foolish environment can damage their child. There is a strong chance that such a child will "inherit" foolishness. Prudent parents will produce prudent children, if the environment is favorable. That child will seek knowledge and make wise decisions. We are the mentors for our children, protecting them, and directing them to the truth! Ensure that you are standing on the firm foundation of faith, so you can support them in their quest for knowledge. Help them find and hold onto Jesus. Faith in the Lord is the way to a crown of righteousness. That is indeed prudent.

SEEK GOD'S FACE

"God be merciful to us and bless us, and cause His face to shine upon us, Selah. That Your way may be known on earth, Your salvation is for all nations." *–Psalm 67:1-2*

Three Things

1. God's mercy and blessing is needed
2. His way must be known for the entire earth
3. His salvation is for all nations

God's mercy and blessing is the endorsement, the anointing that allows us to share His Word. We speak His Word to share His Way on the earth. Scripture reminds us that we are to go into all the world and make disciples. There is no selfishness in God. He expects for His truth to be available to all nations. That is part of His plan.

Are you a stumbling block to God's Word? Does your attitude show on your face when a sermon is not to your liking? Ask God to shine His face upon you and change your heart. Seek His face.

SEEK GOOD FRUIT

"And have no fellowship with the unfruitful works of darkness, but rather expose them." *–Ephesians 5:11*

We often tolerate wrong behavior and scriptural teaching because we seek to remain "humble." A difference in church culture, or a lack of theological understanding is no reason to support darkness. Anything that directs you from the Word of God must be avoided. Scripture reminds us that we were chosen that we might go and bear fruit, and that such fruit would remain. Sharing the gospel is the work that leads to making disciples. Involvement with anything that obscures the light of faith in you obstructs your work. You will then become unfruitful in your work for God, wherever He has assigned you. Sometimes the best fruit is found in places where the trees are protected from contamination. Better soil, better fruit. Where are you planted? Avoid darkness and seek to bear good fruit.

PRIDE: A TOXIC JEWEL

"When pride comes, then comes shame; but with the humble is wisdom." –*Proverbs 11:2*

Three Things

1. Pride is a destructive thing
2. Pride brings shame with it
3. Humility leads to wisdom

So much of our life is spent either living in pride or fighting pride. Comparing ourselves among ourselves brings division, as we begin to resent ourselves. There is no unity among the proud, and pride destroys the beauty of God's peace with resentment. This eventually brings shame for what destructive and prideful hands perform. Scripture reminds us that God resists the proud but gives grace to the humble. A life of humility teaches us to walk the path of peace and brings wisdom beyond what is honored by this world. Satan's pride resulted in his rejection by God. Now he tempts others to fall with him. All for a shiny jewel that has no real worth eternally. A toxic jewel of pride.

JUST ABIDE

"If you abide in Me, and my words abide in you, you will ask what you desire, and it shall be done for you. By this My Father is glorified, that you bear much fruit; so you will be My disciples."
–*John 15:7-8*

From good branches come good fruit. When we abide in Jesus, we become like Him. When His words abide in us, we speak as He does. So, as we grow in Him, our desires become as His. When we ask in accordance with His will, it shall be done. From this, we are able to bear great fruit, because it is from Him, and to Him. Scripture reminds us that we have not because we ask not. But it goes on to speak of asking amiss – for our own selfish desires. The determination to abide in Him pushes out that selfishness. Selfishness is pride. When you are tempted to send a prayer asking for what you know is selfish, just admonish yourself. No pride, just abide.

KEY TO FREEDOM

"For You have delivered my soul from death, my eyes from tears, and my feet from falling. I will walk before the Lord in the land of the living." *–Psalm 116:8-9*

Three Things

1. You have delivered my soul
2. You dried my tears, and steadied me
3. I will walk before the Lord on earth

What a life we lived before the Lord saved us. Our sin brought tears to our eyes and caused us to fall along the path. How glorious that He delivered our soul from eternal death. Is that the reason joy fills our hearts, and we can now dance along the paths that used to stumble us? Rejoice, the scriptures say, and again I say rejoice. For if you walk with joy in the land of the living, someone will ask about your joy. Then you can tell them about the Lord who gives freedom. For whom the Lord sets free is free indeed. Only He has the key.

WATCH YOUR SPIRIT

"The spirit of a man will sustain him in sickness, but who can bear a broken spirit?" *–Proverbs 18:14*

Three Things

1. The spirit strengthens in time of need
2. It will sustain him in sickness
3. A broken spirit leads to collapse

Scripture reminds us that a merry heart does good, like medicine. But a broken spirit dries the bones. The world is filled with those who have received a traumatic blow to their spirit and are a shadow of their former selves. As we see them, we wonder what could make them give up on life so completely? When pain runs that deep, only the Lord can heal the injury. Guard your heart with all diligence and keep on the breastplate of righteousness. In this cruel world, it is better to be careful than to be a casualty. Watch over your spirit.

NO ANXIETY

"In the multitude of my anxieties within me, Your comforts delight my soul." –*Psalm 94:19*

Three Things

1. Life can bring anxiety
2. Anxiety can build up within us
3. The Lord can delightfully comfort

Yes, I know scripture tells us to be anxious for nothing. But in living life, the realities of life can mount up if we allow it. Time spent in the presence of the Lord is multifunctional. It will take your eyes off the problem, strengthen your faith so that you able to do what is needed, and will weaken your pride so that He can go to work through you. When you are weak, He is strong. How glorious to know that weakness is a show of strength for God when you depend upon Him. Be anxious for nothing. Let your faith help you walk past things that used to make you anxious. Cast your cares upon Him.

DAY 108

GRACE IS GOOD

"Therefore take heed to yourselves and to all the flock, among which the Holy Spirit has made you overseer to shepherd the church of God which He purchased with His own blood." –*Acts 20:28*

When criticism comes from church members, it is good to consider what true Pastors must consider. First, they must pay attention to themselves and all the flock. Disregarding themselves can lead to burnout and fatigue. Second, the Holy Spirit made them overseers, not any church board. Third, God purchased the church with His own blood. Therefore, the church is His. It is wise to examine yourself before you release negative opinions about the Pastor, Bishop, Elder, and/or Overseer. Their job is to train up the saints for the work of the ministry. It is a strong possibility that you are being prepared for an office that will use your skills. Are you ready to receive the treatment you give to your Pastor? Show some grace.

APPROACH GENTLY

"By long forbearance a ruler is persuaded, and a gentle tongue breaks a bone." –*Proverbs 25:15*

Three Things

1. Our behavior changes situations
2. Patience and longsuffering persuade rulers
3. Gentle communication breaks resistance

When we experience resistance from a person in charge of a situation in which we are involved, our response and behavior can change the situation. Patience and an attitude of long-suffering is better than angry or insulting words. Patience often brings understanding, and respect. Gentle communication will often break unreasonable resistance from others. It will also bring correction to high emotions, allowing for deeper understanding. Here's something to remember; louder volume leads to anger and resentment. When you brandish your sword, you may find that your "opponent" has a bigger sword. Approach gently.

DAY 110

JESUS PRAYS

"I pray for them. I do not pray for the world but for those whom You have given Me, for they are Yours. And all Mine are Yours, and Yours are mine, and I am glorified in them." *–John 17:9-10*

What a glorious thought. If you belong to Jesus Christ, He prays for you. When you struggle with daily problems – He prays. When your sleep is disturbed by recent events – He prays. When the world brings temptation to your door – He prays. This assurance are words spoken by Jesus, not just reported by another! Now the question emerges: do you belong to Him? Are you seeking safety in your good works, or some "higher power" that has not made itself known? You belong to Him when you make the intelligent choice to accept Him. Salvation is a gift given by grace, but you have to receive it by faith. When He prays, good things happen. Come into His kingdom. I pray that you will.

CONFIDENCE OF GOD

"For God is my King from of old, working salvation in the midst of the earth." –*Psalm 74:12*

Three Things

1. God id my King
2. He has always existed
3. He works salvation on the earth

My God rules the earth and is my King. I honor Him because He is my King and my God. Scripture calls Him the 'Ancient of Days' because He existed before time began. How good to know that His love is with us, even as we fulfill His commandment to go into all the world and make disciples. When we present the gospel, God works salvation. We get to be a part of that miracle. Scripture tells us that the harvest is plentiful, yet the workers are few. When you live righteously, people will be drawn to you. When they get close enough, tell them the secret: Jesus is the Way. Don't be loud. Be confident. God is.

OVERCOMING LOVE

"If the world hates you, you know that it hated Me before it hated you. If you were of the world, the world would love its own. Yet because you are not of the world, but I chose you out of the world, there for the world hates you." –*John 15:18-19*

When you struggle against your circumstances, and adversity seems to pile up through no fault of your own, count it all joy. This light affliction is a backlash against your faith, your prayers, and your love. Quit? Heaven forbids! Tighten up your armor, smile, and continue forward. If you are doing the work assigned to you by God, and you seek righteousness in all you do, the world may indeed hate you. Remember that you were sent into the world to make a difference. Lead by example, speak with love, and work with diligence. As you continue, the love of God residing within you will overcome the world that resists you. Overcome with God's Love.

JUST BE THERE

"The fear of the Lord is to hate evil; pride and arrogance and the evil way and the perverse mouth I hate." –*Proverbs 8:13*

Three Things

1. The fear of the Lord changes attitudes
2. We hate the things God hates
3. We reject perverted speech

The fear of the Lord is the beginning of wisdom, scripture reminds us. As we grow closer to Him, our hearts change. We love the things He loves and hate the things He hates. The work of the Holy Spirit becomes manifest in our behavior, and in our hearts. The words we use, and our attitude toward words used around us also changes. We hate perverse speech, knowing that life and death are in the power of the tongue. Stand in righteousness, beloved. Let the light of His love, and the authority of your faith be shown through your presence. Don't speak. Just Be There.

PREPARE YOUR PRAISE

"All the earth shall worship You and sing praises to You; they shall sing praises to Your name. Selah." –*Psalm 66:4*

Three Things

1. We are created to worship God
2. He is worthy of all praise
3. All the world will sing praises to Him

So much energy is devoted to the negative things that are all around. But our spirit seeks to go beyond the darkness, and to praise the God who created all things. Today we may mourn, but tomorrow praise will pour from our heart. Scripture reminds us that there will come a time when every knee shall bow, and every tongue confess that Jesus Christ is Lord. That time is coming soon. Prepare your hearts and prepare your praise. The new song He gives will ring to the heavens, as you lift up your praise. Practice now. He is coming soon.

DAY 115

WITH ME, OR AGAINST ME?

"He who is not with Me is against Me, and he who does not gather with Me scatters abroad." *–Matthew 12:30*

Regarding spiritual warfare, there are only two sides; you are either for the Lord, or you are against Him. No amount of religious posturing will change the truth of your status. Scripture tells us of the challenge Moses gave to the children of Israel when he declared, "Who is on the Lord's side? Let him come with me." If you are on the Lord's side, there is a call to come out from among those living in darkness and come to the light of truth. Too often today, some declare faith, but display hypocrisy – speaking holiness on Sunday but living in evil the rest of the week. Choose therefore this day whom you will serve. There is no middle group. If you are not with the Lord, you are against Him. Choose wisely.

TEACH THEM GOOD

"A wise son makes a father glad, but a foolish man despises his mother." –*Proverbs 15:20*

Three Things

1. We strive to raise good children
2. A wise son makes a father glad
3. A foolish man despises his mother

How proud we are when our son is wise. His actions make his father stand tall. But a foolish man who despises his mother bring shame to his parents. Scripture reminds us to honor our mother. The love of our mother is seen even by the evilest of men. What type of heart injury can make a man foolish enough to despise his own mother? Raise your children in the nurture and admonition of the Lord. Train them up to go in a good way and warn them about the evils of darkness. Teach them good before the world makes them bad.

STEPS TO FAITH

"The fear of the Lord is the beginning of wisdom; a good understanding have all those who do His commandments. His praise endures forever." –*Psalm 111:10*

Three Things

1. Be wise, fear the Lord
2. Do His commandments with understanding
3. His praise endures forever

Those who seek wisdom will fear the Lord and seek understanding. As they do His commandments, their understanding will deepen. Scripture reminds us to be doers of the Word, and not just hearers only! We learn as we do, and our doing grows faith that we can do all things through Christ who strengthens us. Having overcome, we can rejoice and praise Him forever. Fear God, do His work, and praise Him. All work that grows faith with which to please Him.

GOD'S TREASURE

"But God said to him 'Fool! This night your soul will be required of you; then whose will those things be which you have provided?' So is he who lays up treasure for himself, and is not rich toward God."
–Luke 12:20-21

Everything belongs to God, even our very soul. We are stewards of the treasure and gifts that He places in our lives. Scripture reminds us to lay up treasure in heaven. We do that by investing in the things that bring glory to God. We are to win souls to Christ. Use your gifts to learn how to win souls and to support others who are doing so. No one is impressed by the amount you have stored up for yourself. They can be motivated by the lives you change with such treasures. Consider why God has given you so much more than others. He always has a higher purpose for the gifts He gives. Seek His heart before you build another storehouse. It is not yours.

GODLY CORRECTION

"Foolishness is bound up in the heart of a child; the rod of correction will drive it far from him." –*Proverbs 22:15*

Three Things

1. Foolishness comes naturally
2. Such behavior must be corrected
3. Proper discipline changes behavior

Foolish behavior is not limited to a certain age or education. But it can be dangerous if displayed at the wrong place or time. Mature adults and mature Christians are expected to behave accordingly. When we miss the mark, discipline should be expected. Scripture reminds us that whom God loves, He disciplines. So proper discipline is connected with love, designed to protect and guide us. Scripture says that the fool has said in his heart, "There is no God." That is the type of foolishness in need of correction. Godly correction.

THE BEAUTY OF MERCY

"But the mercy of the Lord is from everlasting to everlasting on those who fear Him, and His righteousness to children's children, to such as keep His covenant, and to those who remember His commandment to do them!" –*Psalm 103:17-18*

Three Things

1. God's mercy is eternal
2. He blesses those who fear Him
3. Keep His covenant and do His commandments

God has special mercies for those who fear Him and do His commandments. For those who keep His covenant, He extends His righteousness even to the children's children. Scripture reminds us that the fear of the Lord is the beginning of wisdom. If you say you love the Lord, why not keep His commandments? Don't just ask God for mercy when times are hard. Realize that God's mercy is at work in your life constantly. That is a beautiful thing. There is a beauty in His mercy.

SPEAK PEACE

"Scoffers set a city aflame, but wise men turn away wrath."
–*Proverbs 29:8*

Three Things

1. Emotion can result in violence
2. Some do not like to be ridiculed
3. Lighting fires lead to greater destruction

School yards use to ring with the statement, "Sticks and stones may break my bones, but words will never hurt me!" Today, it is not words that ring out, but the sound of bullets being sent because of hurtful words. Emotion is often fueled by words. And immature responses to anger can lead to violence. Scripture advises us to bridle our tongue, as it is a fire that can cause great destruction. A sign of maturity is being able to control our tongue. The enemy would have us to "speak our mind." But in certain situations, our minds can mislead us into speaking words that cannot be recaptured. Better to close our mouths and open our ears - we might hear the Holy Spirit say, "Peace".

SEE YOURSELF

"The Lord is high above all nations, His glory above the heavens. Who is like the Lord our God, who dwells on high, who humbles Himself to behold the things that are in the heavens and in the earth?"
–Psalm 113:4-6

Three Things

1. The Lord is high above all nations
2. He dwells above the heavens
3. He beholds all things

There is none like our God. High above all nations, His glory dwells high above the heavens. Yet He humbles Himself to behold all things that are in the heavens and in the earth. Scripture asks, "What is man that You are mindful of him?" Why would a God that created the world give the gift of His Son that we might gain eternal life? It would seem that you are precious in His sight. Maybe it is time for you to clean your mirror, and see what God sees in you.

PRACTICING AMBASSADORS

"Now then, we are ambassadors for Christ, as though God were pleading through us: we implore you on Christ's behalf, be reconciled to God. For He made Him who knew no sin to be sin for us, that we might become the righteousness of God in Him." *–2 Corinthians 5:20-21*

What a sobering thought: we are ambassadors for Christ, working to become the righteousness of God in Him! Knowing that we can no longer "do our own thing", we must take the assignment seriously. We are tasked with representing Christ as we traverse this world. Your work, your words, and your will to obey His Word are all evaluated by the world we seek to win for Him. We do not have to be perfect, but we do have to be willing and available. Our skills have been given to us, and opportunity to serve is everywhere. There is an abundant harvest for those willing to serve. We serve God by serving His people. Start by representing Him in your home. It is good practice.

DAY 124

GET HOLINESS

"For why should you, my son, be enraptured by an immoral woman, and be embraced in the arms of a seductress? –*Proverbs 5:20*

Three Things

1. We want the best for our sons
2. Not being enraptured by immorality
3. Or embraced by seducers

God wants the best for His children. Holiness and purity are what He urges us toward. His Word tells us to walk in the Spirit, and not seek to satisfy the desires of the flesh. That leads to sin, which results in death. Why would you want your children, or yourself, to take that path? Scripture informs us that in God's presence is fulness of joy, at His right hand are pleasures forevermore. Sin is fleeting, God's joy is for eternity. Patience will reveal the truth of this scripture. Draw near to God, and He will draw near to you, bringing a better reward. Immorality is bad; holiness is good. Got it! Go get it!

GOD OUR GUIDE

"For this is God, our God forever and ever; He will be our guide even to death." –*Psalm 48:14*

Three Things

1. When you know God, you know who He is
2. He is unchanging for eternity
3. He will guide us even to death

God will make Himself known to those who seek to know Him. Our spirit communicates to Him when we are not sure how to pray, scripture tells us. When we die, our spirit returns to Him, the God who is the same forever. How comforting to realize that God, who is our Shepherd, will guide us even to death and beyond. Some seek the blessings of God but reject His holiness. Although He is merciful, He is also righteous. It is better that we learn His precepts, obey His commandments, and listen to His voice. If you live on the edge of obedience, just remember: It is a long way down.

FOLLOW THE MAKER

"Then Jesus said to them, "Follow Me, and I will make you become fishers of men." –*Mark 1:17*

No preparation, or qualifying sales talk. Just a straightforward promise wrapped in an invitation. Jesus saw their passion and lifted it to an eternal level. How often do we work on physical activities and not realize that we can apply that skill for the glory of God? When we are ready, the Lord appears with an irresistible invitation. We will have to work to realize it, but the rewards are undeniable. His invitations are not a question such as, "Would you like to?", but a confirmation of what we already have in our heart. It's an invitation that we don't have to pray about. He has been preparing you for this opportunity. Now you enter the next phase of training. Follow Jesus, He knows where your destiny lies. He built it for you.

THE BEST WAY

"In the way of righteousness is life, and in its pathway there is no death." *–Proverbs 12:28*

Three Things

1. We can choose righteousness or sin
2. The way or righteousness is life
3. The wages of sin is death

Pursuing the way or righteousness in this world is difficult and thankless. The resistance against you is only relieved by the enticement of sin available to you. The excitement of a sinful life seems a stark contrast to a life of holiness. But scripture reminds us that our time on earth is short, only vapor. And the wages of sin is death, a death of eternal existence without the presence of God to comfort us. Although the choice between sin and holiness makes perfect sense logically, our soul must weigh in. When the Holy Spirit tugs at your heart, hear Him. His way is the best way.

THE GOOD LIFE

"Whom have I in heaven but You? And there is none upon earth that I desire besides You. My flesh and my heart fail; but God is the strength of my heart and my portion forever." –*Psalm 73:25-26*

Three Things

1. I have no one in heaven but You
2. You are all I desire on earth
3. God is my strength and my portion

God is the only one in heaven who hears my call and inclines His ear. Above all the things earth may offer, I need the love of God. As my flesh grows older, God gives strength to my heart. Scripture declares that I know my redeemer lives, and I have reached that realization. I know that He will redeem me in the end, and I will dwell in His presence forever. Others may seek silver and gold, but my desired portion is Him. Until then, I live for Him, worship Him, and speak of Him. That is a good life.

A BETTER USE

"If you really fulfill the royal law according to the scripture, "You shall love your neighbor as yourself", you do well; but if you show partiality, you commit sin, and are convicted by the law as transgressors. For whoever shall keep the whole law, and yet stumble in one point, he is guilty of all." –*James 2:8-10*

Striving to fulfill the commandments found in scripture is a dangerous venture. For if you fulfill one, and yet fail at one point at another, you are guilty of transgression for all. With our inability to obey God, how can we show partiality to others, as though we can judge their goodness? Do we not have enough work to do on ourselves that we should reject another? The grace of God brings salvation to those of us who could not even fulfill God's law. The perfection of Jesus Christ became our covering, by which we could be accepted by God. Knowing that, our hands would be better used to praise the Lord and not point out others we dislike.

PLEASE THE KING

"The king's wrath is like the roaring of a lion, but his favor is like dew on the grass." –*Proverbs 19:12*

Three Things

1. Those in authority can respond emotionally
2. When angry, they may yell
3. When pleased, they show favor

Many have worked for an emotional leader who seems to change like the weather, sometimes for no apparent reason. Scripture reminds us that the heart of the king is in the hand of God, who turns it wherever He wishes. When we work for the glory of God, we do not have to fear the changes of heart. God smiles at excellence, and rewards diligence. When your work ethic is guided by your faith, you strive for better each day. Even when your leader is pleased, work to represent the King of kings. Favor of earthly kings is pleasant, but it cannot match the words from the Lord – "Well done, My good and faithful servant." Please the King!

SHARING THE ANOINTING

"You love righteousness and hate wickedness; therefore God, Your God, has anointed You with the oil of gladness more than Your companions. *–Psalm 45:7*

Three Things

1. Love righteousness and hate wickedness
2. God Himself will anoint you
3. You will be distinct from others

Written to the King of Kings, we understand that the love of righteousness, and hatred of wickedness led to an anointing from God. As the Body of Christ, does not the oil flow down to us as it did down Aaron's robe? When you clearly remember the salvation you have received, the oil of gladness will enlighten your soul. The joy of the Lord, which is your strength, will bring a radiant smile to your face. Perhaps it will be that your companions will ask the reason for your faith. Scripture reminds us to be ready to give a reason for the hope that guides us into our faith for the future. Be ready to share the blessing of the gospel. Share the anointing.

DON'T MISS IT

"Watch therefore, for you know neither the day nor the hour in which the Son of Man is coming." *–Matthew 25:13*

It seems like a long time to wait for Jesus to return. And the world gets more wicked by the day. But He did tell us to occupy until He came back. So, we will continue to do the work set forth until we hear the trumpets blowing. That should give us little time for gossip, fornication, or any of the other sins that seem to occupy the attention of the world. That is the point. If you don't know when He is coming, you just might behave. Spend time in the scripture, and in prayer. Commit your ways to the Lord, and He will make your paths straight. But watch and pray, He could arrive any day. This is one event you do not want to miss.

GET UP, LAZY ONES

"The lazy man says, 'There is a lion in the road, a fierce lion is in the streets!' As a door turns on its hinges, so does the lazy man on his bed." –*Proverbs 26:13-14*

Three Things

1. Laziness prevents one from working
2. Excuses are easily offered
3. Sleepiness makes it hard to get up

Laziness is a learned behavior that is often tolerated by others, even as it is perfected by the lazy ones. No excuse is sufficient to support one who is able but allows laziness to rob them of their resources. Scripture reminds us that one who will not work should not eat. But laziness comes in many forms. The believer who is too lazy to study the Bible for themselves are unable to digest the Word of God. Although the harvest is plentiful, lazy hands can do little to lift up the Lord before this dying world. Wake up, get up, you lazy ones. There is work to do!

YOU WILL SEE

"Wait on the Lord; be of good courage, and He shall strengthen your heart; wait, I say, on the Lord." *–Psalm 27:14*

Three Things

1. Some things are worth waiting for
2. Wait patiently with courage
3. The Lord will strengthen your heart

When tragedy is headed your way, it is natural to want help right now. The idea of waiting on the Lord makes no sense. But it takes courage to wait when trouble threatens to overcome you. Faith is the only thing that assures you that He will come through on time. Scripture tells us that He will never leave us, nor forsake us. When we realize that He is with us when we need Him most, our heart is strengthened. Then we are no longer waiting for Him to arrive. We are now waiting to see how He will turn the situation around. If you have not experienced that yet – just wait.

OPEN YOUR GIFT

"Do not neglect the gift that is in you, which was given to you by prophecy with the laying on of the hands of the eldership. Meditate on these things; give yourself entirely to them, that your progress may be evident to all." *–1 Timothy 4:14-15*

Every gift is given by God, but eventually recognized by man. Godly leadership may speak of those gifts they see in you, and even pray that you will exercise them for the glory of God. But until you realize those gifts, carefully consider how they are to be used, and begin to use them, such gifts are wasted. Every gift God gives is practical as well as spiritual. Scripture reminds us that He knows how to give good gifts to His children. So, think about the gift you have been given. Share that gift with all who need the comfort and strength that God has provided through you. Open the gift. Don't waste it.

GUARD WISDOM

"She is more precious than rubies, and all the things you may desire cannot compare with her." *–Proverbs 3:15*

Three Things

1. Wisdom must be considered
2. She is more precious than rubies
3. More than anything you desire

When the subject of riches comes up, seldom is the gift of wisdom mentioned. We want the universally valued things like gold, silver, and other things that the world can see. But wisdom cannot be seen or displayed for others to admire. Only the result of wisdom applied can be seen, and that result often takes a while before it emerges. Scripture reminds us not to cast our pearls before swine. They will only destroy them, and you. If you have attained the blessing of wisdom, be wise. Refrain from letting everyone know that wisdom is in your possession. Some things of value must be guarded.

SPEAK WHAT SHOULD BE HEARD

"We have heard with our ears, O God, our fathers have told us, the deeds You did in their days, in days of old." *–Psalm 44:1*

Three Things

1. God's deeds must be told
2. Those that hear them will remember
3. The goodness of the past forms the memories of the future

So easily we remember the themes we have heard our fathers speak. We experience excitement as they recount important things from their past. How often do fathers share the wonders that God has worked in their lives now? How strong would the faith of a son be, who hears how God has blessed his own father? No longer would such things exist only in the pages of scripture, but a life of blessing from God would become real. Fathers, are you aware of the Seeds that God, our Father, has made manifest in your lives? Speak that in the hearing of your sons. Those truths must be heard. Speak them.

FAILURE IS NOT AN OPTION

"I have fought the good fight, I have finished the race, I have kept the faith." *–2 Timothy 4:7*

At the end of tough circumstances, even as you emerge from the challenge bruised and dirty, it is satisfying to report - "It is finished." Jesus provides the perfect model as He took on increasingly difficult challenges yet kept His determination to complete the task. Even while hanging on the cross in agony. His love for humanity came through, as He declared, "Forgive them, for they know not what they do!" Whether it is a physical battle, a running contest, or a spiritual conflict, we must persevere. Even when resistance comes from every side, and all seems hopeless – stand strong. God, who seems to make a way when there is no way, will come through for you. He cannot fail you – don't fail Him. Failure is not an option.

LOVE CHOICE

"Hatred stirs up strife, but love covers all sins." –*Proverbs 10:12*

Three Things

1. We can approach everything with either love or hatred
2. Hatred stirs up strife
3. Love covers all sins

Our approach to people and situations in life depends on the decisions of our heart. If we have decided to hate them that will lead to strife or even death. But if we decide to love, we develop the ability to forgive, and peace begins to spread. Scripture reminds us that we are known by our love if we follow Christ. Emotion unchecked can result in regrettable conditions. Anger grows into hatred, which develops into rage. Before you allow that to destroy your soul, know that you are indeed your brother's keeper. Lead with love. It will shorten every battle. It is the best choice.

A GLORIOUS ANSWER

"Hear my prayer, O Lord, and let my cry come to You! Do not hide Your face from me in the day of trouble; incline Your ear to me; in the day that I call, answer me speedily." –*Psalm 102:1-2*

Three Things

1. Hear my prayer in the day of trouble
2. Do not hide your face from me
3. When I call, answer me quickly

Trouble wears on the soul, and even the most urgent prayers seem to be unheard by God at times. We seek His face, that we can be certain that He hears us. Scripture reminds us that when we call to Him, our God will answer. Furthermore, He will show us great and mighty things that we do not know. God knows what is best for us. So, as He prepares the answer for us, He is also preparing us for that answer. Be patient and continue working. The result will bring joy to your heart and glory to God. He always brings a glorious answer.

NO OTHER GOD

"O Lord God of hosts, who is mighty like You, O Lord? Your faithfulness also surrounds You." –*Psalm 89:8*

Three Things

1. The Lord is God of hosts
2. He is mighty beyond all others
3. His faithfulness surrounds Him

He cannot be compared to any other. The Lord is God of hosts. Strong and mighty beyond all others, scripture reminds us that He alone is God Almighty. His faithfulness surrounds Him like a robe. Could that be the train that fills the Temple? His glory is from everlasting to everlasting. Yet there remain some who do not believe. We must tell them of God's Truth before their time of judgment. The fool has said in his heart, "There is no God." Seek Him while He may be found. Time grows short. Exalt Him in your heart and proclaim Him throughout this land. He is God. There is no other!

DAY 142

PREACH AND LIVE

"Preach the word! Be ready in season and out of season. Convince, rebuke, exhort, with all longsuffering and teaching." –*2 Timothy 4:2*

How you feel doesn't matter, nor the responses you get afterward. We cannot let the opinions, or attitudes of others prevent us from sharing the Word of God. If you trust in the Lord, trust also in His Word. There is no room for doubt or fear that changes faith. Hear the prompting of the Holy Spirit, then share the good news. Preaching does not have to be a show. It is a proclaiming of what is true. You can do it one on one. Just do it. There is no time or place for this, be ready when the opportunity arrives. You don't have to knock them over with your volume or your vocabulary. Persuade them with your love and convince them with the truth. Rebuke them for their behavior and exhort them to accept the Lord's precious gift. Preach it, then live it.

EVIL IS NOT FOR YOU

"Do not be envious of evil men, nor desire to be with them; for their heart devises violence, and their lips speak of troublemaking."
–*Proverbs 24:1-2*

Three Things

1. Avoid the presence of evil men
2. They devise violence
3. They speak troublemaking

Evil men have nothing to admire. Avoid their company, and do not desire fellowship with them. In their hearts, they plan violence, and they speak only of troublemaking. Scripture reminds us that from the abundance of the heart, the mouth speaks. When you remain in such environments, you will either become like them or fall victim to their evil ways. Choose righteousness and walk in your integrity. Leave evil to its own reward. They will reap what they sow. You just keep your hand on the plow, and sow faith. The harvest will be plentiful, and pure.

HIS HANDS WORK

"The works of His hands are verity and justice; all His precepts are sure. They stand fast forever and ever, and are done in truth and uprightness." *–Psalm 111:7-8*

Three Things

1. The works of God's hands are truth and justice
2. His laws are sure, done in uprightness
3. They will stand fast forever

The works of God's hands are truth and justice. Some question that, not realizing that they receive the result of their own work. Scripture reminds us that we will reap what we sow. God forgives, but we must pay the price for our actions. God's laws are eternal, crafted in truth and done in uprightness. God is never wrong and never late. Although we refuse to accept the things that happen in our lives, God has a purpose for it all. This light affliction that life brings is but for a season. A greater reward comes behind. That is also a work of God's hands. His hands are working on you even now.

SIMPLE IS BETTER

"But I fear, lest somehow, as the serpent deceived Eve by his craftiness, so your minds may be corrupted from the simplicity that is in Christ." *–2 Corinthians 11:3*

It is simple. God loves us. Christ died for us. We accept Him. We live for Him. Eternity in heaven is ours. Yet we complicate it to make more than we are. So much of scripture will not truly be understood until we get to heaven. Christ gave His life that we might reunite with the Father. Satan uses every device to separate us from the Father, and from each other as the Body of Christ. I have even seen Pastors argue about the "credentialing" differences in their seminary training. Such appeals to the pride of man reduces our effective work for the Kingdom of God. By faith we have been saved, and by obedience we walk in this world for God. Let me encourage us all to return to the simplicity that is in Christ. Simple is better.

WORK IS LOVE

"She stretches out her hands to the distaff, and her hands hold the spindle. She extends her hand to the poor, yes, she reaches out her hands to the needy." *–Proverbs 31:19-20*

Three Things

1. The work of our hands reveals our heart
2. A woman of God works hard
3. She helps the poor and the needy

Among the many characteristics of a virtuous woman, a woman of God, is the tendency to get her hands involved in the work. Scripture reminds us that Jesus works on our behalf, and that the Father also works. Many of us remember the hands of our mother as she worked for us. Preparing meals, washing clothes, cleaning the house – it was a labor of love. And if the work was done with a song or a smile, it made it even more precious. A woman or a man who works teaches valuable lessons to their children. Work is love.

SUCH MAGNIFICENCE

"O Lord, how manifold are Your works! In wisdom You have made them all. The earth is full of Your possessions." –*Psalm 104:24*

Three Things

1. God's works are manifold
2. Wisdom was an instrument to create them
3. Earth is full of His possessions

Behold the glory of God on every level of existence. His works are manifold and mighty. Scripture reminds us that we cannot go anywhere to escape Him. Yet there is nothing wasted or haphazard in all creation. His wisdom was used to create the tiniest detail. Should we live throughout eternity, we would be unable to see and experience all that God possesses on this earth. The earth is His, and the fullness thereof. Consider the work of His hands in you, for you are fearfully and wonderfully made! Such a miracle that He would create from dust His image to live on this magnificent earth, and in the glory of heaven.

DAY 148

POWER TO DO IT

"Therefore, when they had come together, they asked Him, saying, "Lord, will You at this time restore the kingdom to Israel?" And He said to them, "It is not for you to know times or seasons which the Father has put in His own authority. But you shall receive power when the Holy Spirit has come upon you; and you shall be witnesses to Me in Jerusalem, and in all Judea and Samaria, and to the end of the earth." *–Acts 1:6-8*

Now is the time to be about our Father's business. We hear of wars and rumors of wars. All time points to the return of Jesus Christ. Rather than trying to calculate the season by the obvious, we must declare the obvious to the world. Many still do not know Jesus, although they have heard of Him. Faith in Him changes lives. We don't need bigger churches. We need bigger voices to speak truth to this sleeping, busy world. Ask for forgiveness, ask for salvation. Ask for direction to change your heart and mind. Then ask for power through the Holy Spirit to tell somebody about Jesus. Then go do it.

DAY 149

STRONG WISDOM

"Wisdom strengthens the wise more than ten rulers of the city."
–*Ecclesiastes 7:19*

Three Things

1. We need strength to survive
2. Wisdom strengthens those who are wise
3. Ten rulers add strength to the city

Weakness can lead to destruction, so we seek those things that strengthen us. A city may have ten rulers with skills and knowledge sufficient to protect them from attack. Scripture reminds us that a wise man increases strength. Whether physical, intellectual, or spiritual, greater wisdom leads to greater strength. For us who believe, we are to be strong in the Lord, and in the power of His might. As knowledge of the Lord is the beginning of knowledge, it is wise to grow closer to Him. Our strong is in Him.

WILLING STUDENT

"Teach me, O Lord, the way of Your statutes, and I shall keep it to the end. Give me understanding, and I shall keep Your law; indeed, I shall observe it with my whole heart." –*Psalm 119:33-34*

Three Things

1. Teaching and understanding come from God
2. Statutes and laws must be kept
3. Observe it with your whole heart

When the Lord teaches, there is no doubt regarding its truth. His statutes and laws cannot be kept unless it is understood. Scripture advises us to study to show ourselves approved by God and man. God does not expect blind obedience when dealing with His Word. He is pleased when we ask the Holy Spirit to illuminate the meaning of the words. Having faith that God will do so, pleases Him. It also allows us to live rightly, and rightly divide the Word of Truth. Seek Him with your whole heart and live as a willing student.

STILL SERVING

"Then the seventy returned with joy, saying, "Lord, even the demons are subject to us in Your name", and He said to them, "I saw Satan fall like lightning from heaven. Behold, I give you the authority to trample on serpents and scorpions, and over all the power of the enemy, and nothing shall by any means hurt you. Nevertheless, do not rejoice in this, that the spirits are subject to you, but rather rejoice because your names are written in heaven." *–Luke 10:17-20*

He has overcome the world, and the battle is not against flesh and blood. The enemy delights in confusing communication and creating chaos. We are one body, the Body of Christ, with diverse abilities. It is time to unite against our common enemy (Satan) and deny him further access to damage our work for the Lord. As we honor and recognize the service of all veterans who have stood to protect others, let us remember that we all still serve. We serve the Lord by serving His people. Thank you for your service.

GUARD YOUR HEART

"The heart knows its own bitterness, and a stranger does not share its joy." –*Proverbs 14:10*

Three Things

1. Strong emotion is personal
2. Bitterness is kept close to the heart
3. Strangers do not share every joy

Life brings every situation that our heart experiences. Whether deep pain leading to bitterness, or blessings that carry great joy; it all goes to the heart. Scripture reminds us to guard our heart with all diligence, for from it flows the issues of life. To open our heart to strangers, or those who mean to harm us, is foolish. Testing the spirits will increase our discernment as they relate to Jesus. But most often it is better to put your trust in Jesus. He will not share your concerns or joys with those seeking to destroy you. Love them, but do not give a gossiper more ammunition. If you hurt, only the Lord can heal. So, guard your heart; that takes longer to heal.

FIREPROOF WORKS

"Let Your work appear to Your servants, and Your glory to their children. And let the beauty of the Lord our God be upon us, and establish the work of our hands for us; yes, establish the work of our hands." *–Psalm 90:16-17*

Three Things

1. We need to see God's work and His glory
2. We want the beauty of the Lord
3. God can establish the work of our hands

God's handiwork can be seen by all. The majesty of the heavens, the power of the sea, and the laugh of a child are all God's work. We pray that the beauty of the Lord will be upon us as we labor for Him. Scripture reminds us that God is always at work, so He understands the work we do. But if we labor selfishly, without God in the midst, we labor in vain. With God in the work, He will establish the work of our hands. Does your work glorify God? Only that which is done for Christ will last. Selfish works will burn like hay and stubble. Make sure that your work is fireproof.

PHONY FAITH FAILS

"And then many will be offended, will betray one another, and will hate one another. Then many false prophets will rise up and deceive many. And because lawlessness will abound, the love of many will grow cold. But he who endures to the end shall be saved." –*Matthew 24:10-13*

Could it be that we are seeing this come to pass today? Messages that stir the heart, tickle the ears, and dull our perception are well-received. We hear that true Christians are always happy, never sick, and reject suffering. So, we exist in a make-believe world until reality and truth emerges to remove our rose-colored glasses. Scripture reminds us that our faith is strengthened through adversity. Wisdom comes as we go through trials and acquire knowledge. We must live life and speak truth. Faith is an action word that is exercised, not declared. Avoid the easy, phony faith that so easily flows from the mouth of many seeking to fill you with emotion, not truth. If you have not tested faith in real life, it will fail you.

HALF THE BATTLE

"The horse if prepared for the day of battle, but deliverance is of the Lord." –*Proverbs 21:31*

Three Things

1. The day of battle will come
2. We must prepare for it
3. The Lord will deliver us

We cannot ignore the fact that a spiritual battle rages all around us. We see the results of it as casualties mount, and lives are destroyed. We would be foolish not to prepare to face enemies seen and unseen – that is our responsibility as believers. Scripture reminds us that we are to be sober, vigilant, as our enemy prowls about seeking to devour us. Walking circumspectly, fully alert to the pitfalls of sin and pride, clad in the full armor of God will protect us as we labor for His Kingdom. Have faith that the Lord will deliver those whom He loves. Trials will make you strong. His love has made you free. That is half the battle. Conquering fear is the rest.

WEAR IT WELL

"Therefore, as the elect of God, holy and beloved, put on tender mercies, kindness, humility, meekness, longsuffering; bearing with one another, and forgiving one another, if anyone has a complaint against another; even as Christ forgave you, so you also must do. But above all these things put on love, which is the bond of perfection."
–*Colossians 3:12-14*

They shall know us by our love, one for another, scripture reminds us. None of the behavior mentioned is possible without the power of the Holy Spirit. If we are dressed in tender mercies, kindness, and so forth, He alone tailors it to our sufficiency. Should we try to put any of these precious garments on ourselves, the result is ill-fitting, clumsy, and embarrassing. The foundation is love, flowing from our heart by the power of the Holy Spirit. Covering up as a robe of righteousness, it reaches out to the heart of those who have not seen the love of Christ. You have been chosen to wear it – Wear it well!

AVOID SCAMS

"One who increases his possessions by usury and extortion gathers it for him who will pity the poor." –*Proverbs 28:8*

Three Things

1. Evil people prosper by evil means
2. God judges and will repay deception
3. Righteous will bless others and be blessed

Those with evil intentions will seek riches by mistreating and cheating the poor. Scripture reminds us that the treasure of the wicked are stored up for the righteous. So, God may seem to tolerate the temporary abuse of His righteous Ones, to give time for the treasury to grow. That also gives the targets of such tactics to gain wisdom and avoid people who use them. Being a godly person does not mean that we should lower our defenses against scams or crooked individuals. God's money requires good stewards. Don't let greed, or misplaced trust make you lose what is entrusted to you. If it seems too good to be true – avoid it.

REPENT

"The Lord is merciful and gracious, slow to anger, and abounding in mercy. He will not always strive with us, nor will He keep His anger forever." *–Psalm 103:8-9*

Three Things

1. The Lord deals with us daily
2. He is gracious, slow to anger, and abounding in mercy
3. There is a limit to His patience

Something is wrong with mankind. The Lord has patiently dealt with us daily for thousands of years. We sin against Him, destroy His handiwork, and disrespect His Word. Our heart finds ever more ways to turn against God. Scripture reminds us that our heart is more desperately wicked than we could ever know. Yet the Lord, our God, has given us His Son to bring us to eternal salvation. His voice gently urges us to repent and seek His face. Some have said that a merciful God would not destroy even a sinful nation. Do you hear the voices of Sodom and Gomorrah? Repent.

LISTEN TO THE TEACHER

"These things we also speak, not in words which man's wisdom teaches but which the Holy Spirit teaches, comparing spiritual things with spiritual." *–1 Corinthians 2:13*

The greatest wisdom is that which comes from God. He has created everything, and yet remains in control of this world. Do not be confused by the chaos you see today. Scripture reminds us that God is not the author of confusion. We speak what we know, and we live the way we know. In the end, our character is seen in what we do. As the Holy Spirit teaches us to learn of spiritual things, we first compare it to things that are not spiritual, and then begin to discern the spiritual truths. This process is gradual. We learn to hear His voice; then we learn to speak what He teaches. Then we begin, in obedience, to walk according to what we have been taught. Listen closely, the Teacher is teaching.

TEACHERS WARN

"Lest aliens be filled with your wealth, and your labors go to the house of a foreigner; and you mourn at last, when your body and your flesh are consumed, and say: "How I have hated instruction, and my heart despised correction!" –*Proverbs 5:10-12*

Three Things

1. People will take advantage of you
2. Even your death will bring no comfort
3. Give heed to instruction and correction

Those who ignore the wisdom of good teachers will suffer because of it later. Bad decisions may bring financial loss, with strangers claiming the results of your labor. Even sickness and death will not comfort you. Instead, remorse will come as you consider your refusal to learn. This is a serious thought to ponder now. Pay attention to the wisdom of good teachers who try to instruct or correct you. They are warning you.

CAUSE ME

"Cause me to hear Your lovingkindness in the morning, for in You do I trust; cause me to know the way in which I should walk, for I lift my soul up to you." –*Psalm 143:8*

Three Things

1. You can cause me to hear and to know
2. I will hear Your lovingkindness, and know the way I should walk
3. I lift up my soul for your guidance

Some things I have learned along the way, but I need the Lord to cause me to grow closer to Him. To hear His lovingkindness in the gently morning breeze that carries the song of birds praising God in the trees. To nudge me in the right direction as I walk along the paths of life. Scripture reminds us that we will hear a voice behind us telling us to go to the left or the right. When our soul is cast down with the heaviness of doubt, lift up your soul to Him. He is able to cause you to live with Joy.

MORE THAN BLOOD

"Then His mother and brothers came to Him, and could not approach Him because of the crowd. And it was told Him by some, who said, "Your mother and Your brothers are standing outside, desiring to see You." But He answered and said to them, "My mother and My brothers are these who hear the Word of God and do it." *–Luke 8:19-21*

Was this a social rebuke, or a spiritual reality? Jesus marked out a clear dividing line that was not based on bloodlines or physical DNA. Crowds had come to hear Him, and Jesus gave a clear message to them as well. They must not simply hear the Word of God but must also do it. Scripture reminds us that man shall not live by bread alone, but by every word that proceeds out of the mouth of God. God's word is life, but is designed to be applied to our lives, performed in response to our circumstances, and vigorously exercised daily. We are connected to the Lord, not by bloodline, but by faith and obedience. Gather around family, God is speaking. We have work to do.

HERE I AM, LORD

"Help, Lord, for the godly man ceases! For the faithful disappear from among the sons of men. They speak idly everyone with his neighbor; with flattering lips and a double heart they speak." –*Psalm 12:1-2*

Three Things

1. We need God's help when godliness ceases
2. When the faithful are gone, we see it
3. When idle and dishonest speech abounds, we cry out

What a tragedy when we must call on the Lord to bring back godly men. When faithfulness is not present and all seem to speak with lies and deceit, we can either accept that as a painful reality or stand above the rest in our own conduct. Scripture reminds us to seek the Lord while He may be found. If His eyes run to and fro seeking the righteous, make certain that He can find you standing with the godly ones. When He calls, respond, "Here I am, Lord."

DAY 164

BE EXCEEDINGLY GLAD

"Let all those who seek You rejoice and be glad in You; and let those who love Your salvation say continually, "Let God be magnified."
–*Psalm 70:4*

Three Things

1. Some seek the Lord for salvation
2. Let them rejoice and be glad in Him
3. Let all magnify the Lord

When you need the Lord, seek Him diligently. Scripture reminds us that if you seek Him, you will find Him. He came to seek and to save that which was lost. Now we can rejoice in the fact of our salvation. Take time to love Him, to remember the worth of your salvation. He purchased your life with His own blood, so let us magnify Him. We can love Him by our obedience and by our diligent work to serve Him right where we are. Life here on earth is short. Use that time wisely. Praise the Lord for His grace and mercy. Be exceedingly glad that you belong to Him.

KEEP YOUR BAGS PACKED

"And as they went to tell His disciples, behold, Jesus met them, saying, "Rejoice!" So they came and held Him by the feet and worshiped Him. Then Jesus said to them, "Do not be afraid. Go and tell My brethren to go to Galilee, and there they will see Me."
–*Matthew 28:9-10*

With anticipation, we run from one place to another seeking Jesus. So many gatherings declare that Jesus is in their midst yet provide only emotion and promises. Could it be possible that Jesus may be where He is needed most? In this instance, Jesus directs His brethren to go to Galilee. Maybe He is directing you to your place of work, your business, or even your own home. No matter where He sends you, He will go with you. Consider the fact that others need to see Jesus in you. Now is the time for you to spend time in His presence and allow Him to guide and prepare you for the tasks ahead. Be assured that He will meet us at the right time and place. Just be ready to go as He directs. Keep a bag packed for the journey. When you arrive, you will see Him there.

DRAW CLOSE TO JESUS

"Many entreat the favor of the nobility, and every man is a friend to one who gives gifts. All the brothers of the poor hate him; how much more do his friends go far from him! He may pursue them with words, yet they abandon him." –*Proverbs 19:6-7*

Three Things

1. Riches and social status matter to some
2. Friends abound when you provide gifts
3. People hate the poor and run from them

When asked about the poor, scripture reminds us that the poor will always be with us. But we know that society differentiates on the basis of social status and financial circumstances. Yet it is the heart that matters most. The faith that one holds allows for the love deposited in the heart to guide both our actions, and our relationships with those who are rich or poor. When our friends and family run away from us, run to Jesus. He is a friend that sticks closer than a brother and will in no way cast you out. It is a cold world out there. Draw closer to Jesus.

GOD ON YOUR SIDE

"If it had not been the God who was on our side, when man rose up against us, then they would have swallowed us alive; when their wrath was kindled against us." –*Psalm 124:2-3*

Three Things

1. The Lord is on your side
2. Your enemies seek to destroy you
3. The Lord protects you

Spiritual battles rise around you, and enemies rage against you. It may seem at times that there is no safe haven for you. It is then that God provides a shield for you, allowing you to perform the work He sends for you to do. Scripture reminds us that when the enemy comes against us like a flood, God will raise up a standard against him. So be brave and unafraid, if you are engaged in the righteous work of the Lord. The enemy will come, but his weapons will not prosper. But declare to all who will hear, "If it had not been for the Lord who is on my side."

CHECK YOUR HEART

"For he is not a Jew who is one outwardly, nor is circumcision that which is outward in the flesh; but he is a Jew who is one inwardly; and circumcision is that of the heart, in the Spirit, not in the letter; whose praise is not from men but from God." –*Romans 2:28-29*

This insight applies to Christians as well. Our outward appearance, speaking church language, and presenting ourselves as holy does not always reflect what is in our heart. Scripture reminds us that while man looks on the outward appearance, God looks on the heart. It is a good exercise to ask God to clean those things of darkness, anything that is now pleasing to Him, from our heart. That should be daily work, since opportunities to sin are all around us. But if we strive toward righteousness, we avoid the pride that is easy to exhibit outwardly. After all, it is not about you. God tells us to be holy as He is holy. Acting holy does not make us holy. Check your heart to determine the level of holiness that resides within.

LAZY IS NOT FOR YOU

"The lazy man buries his hand in the bowl; it wearies him to bring it back to his mouth." –*Proverbs 26:15*

Three Things

1. Laziness destroys initiative
2. It can become extreme
3. Some are too lazy to feed themselves

I trust that Solomon was using this as an illustration regarding laziness. I could not imagine anyone too lazy to eat. Scripture declares that one who does not work should not eat. Working is a cure for laziness. We must eat to live. So, if we work to eat, we will not be lazy. Unfortunately, some who claim the name of Christ have used their faith to avoid the hard work of performing their job, paying their bills, or keeping their body in reasonable physical shape. When they reach a point of near disaster, then they begin to pray for a miracle. We were not built to be lazy. God builds excellence but expects us to maintain what He has given us. Represent Him well by working as unto the Lord in all you do. Let others be lazy. That is not for you.

IF THEY CAN PRAISE

"Praise Him, you heavens of heavens, and you waters above the heavens! Let them praise the name of the Lord, for He commanded and they were created." –*Psalm 148:4-5*

Three Things

1. There are heavens and waters above the heavens
2. They all praise the Lord
3. At His command they were created

We wonder at the magnificence of the heavens above and seek shelter in the face of storms. Yet we often forget the same Lord who created them also created us. Scripture reminds us that should we fail to honor the Lord, the rocks will cry out. Disobedience and pride can get in the way of our worship, He is worthy of being praised. Even as we rejected Him, He gave His life on the cross to save us. Let not a busy, selfish life prevent us from praising the One who gave us eternal life. Praise Him loudly if you wish, quietly if you must – but praise Him. If the heavens can praise Him, surely, we can.

SHARE THE RICHES

"For the Scripture says, "Whoever believes on Him will not be put to shame." For there is no distinction between Jew and Greek, for the same Lord over all is rich to all who call upon Him." *–Romans 10:11-12*

Believing on Him is the common ground, for all who enter heavens' gates. Although we come from different starting points, we traveled the road in Him, to reach His throne because of Him. The enemy seeks to divide, but Jesus came to seek and to save that which was lost. And that is all of us. So, understand that true believers in Him will not have to be ashamed of their faith. They will see Christ in the day's eternal. Whether now or then, the same God is Lord of all. So, if they do not know Jesus, share the truth with them in love. You may be the one they trust to believe in Him. Some plant, some water, and God gets the increase. Tell them whom to call upon. Share the riches.

A BETTER PATH

"For her house leads down to death, and her paths to the dead; none who go to her return, nor do they regain the paths of life." –*Proverbs 2:18-19*

Three Things

1. Following immorality is dangerous
2. In that house is death
3. The path to death is not the path of life

Seeking a life of riotous living, and pleasures of the flesh is a path that leads to death. When immorality is in the forefront, darkness is all around. Unfortunately, when you reach the point when the wages of your sin are paid, it's too late to take another path. Begin today. Ponder the path you are on and decide to move to the path of life. Change your mind and change your direction. God has promised you a better future, but only if you are obedient to take a better path. You have resolved to improve yourself so many times before. Place yourself in God's hands. He will set you on a path that cannot fail. The path of righteousness. A better path.

RIGHTEOUS BLESSINGS

"For the Lord is righteous, He loves righteousness; His countenance beholds the upright." *–Psalm 11:7*

Three Things

1. The Lord is righteous
2. He loves righteousness
3. His face turns toward the upright

Among the strong characteristics we know, God is righteous. His judgment reflects that righteousness, balanced by His grace. He loves those who are righteous, noting that such are upright in their walk with Him. Scripture notes that the eyes of the Lord run to and fro throughout the earth to show Himself strong on behalf of those whose heart is loyal to Him. When you are loyal, you are upright in your faith. God notices that and turns His face toward you. Such favor can only come from pleasing a righteous God. If you seek the grace of God, start by being righteous and upright. In due season, God's countenance will shine upon you. Stand upright, your righteous blessings are coming.

FAITHFUL VIGILANCE

"Be sober, be vigilant; because your adversary the devil walks about like a roaring lion, seeking whom he may devour. Resist him, steadfast in the faith, knowing that the same sufferings are experienced by your brotherhood in the world." –*1 Peter 5:8-9*

Carelessness in your walk can lead to being a victim of the enemy, who is constantly seeking to kill, steal, and destroy your effectiveness in this world. He uses weapons of deceit and temptation to hinder the progress of believers who strive to grow closer to the Lord. Resist any attempt to lure you from the path that God has placed you. You are not alone in this fight, but society would like to convince you that such things as kindness, holiness, and faith are not acceptable in this modern world. Reject their rejection and continue in the faith. Serve the Lord with your gifts and spend time in His presence. God's approval is more crucial than man's acceptance. Be faithful and vigilant.

SHORT LIFE OR LONG LIFE

"The fear of the Lord prolongs days, but the years of the wicked will be shortened." –*Proverbs 10:27*

Three Things

1. Your attitude affects the length of your life
2. God fearing people live longer
3. Wicked people die sooner

Whom you serve affects the quality and the length of your life here on earth. Those who are wicked and rebellious against the Lord face resistance. Scripture notes that the way of the transgressor is hard. Those who fear, and serve God receive the blessings of the Lord, to include longevity. Not so for those of wicked intent. Their lives will be shortened, as well as filled with tribulation! Since the spirit of man is eternal, how can I make such a statement? When the wicked are on earth, they are in the presence of God, and have opportunity to accept salvation before their time on earth comes to an end. Should their rebelliousness lead them to reject this free gift from God, they will spend eternity without God. That is true death. Spiritual death. Accept Christ and live a long life in the presence of Almighty God.

LIFT HIM UP!

"Oh, give thanks to the Lord! Call upon His name; make known His deeds among the peoples!" –*Psalm 105:1*

Three Things

1. Give thanks to the Lord
2. Call upon His name
3. Tell everyone what He has done

Consider what God has done for you. Call out to Him in prayer and thanksgiving. You have not seen the full extent of what God can do. Scripture states that eyes have not seen, nor ears heard the things that God has prepared for those who love Him. Go ahead and tell others of the work that God has done in your life. Don't wait to receive the greater measure of your blessings. Whet the appetite of all that would hear, so they also would desire more of the Lord. The Lord has said that if He were lifted up, He would draw all men to Himself. Lift Him up, that others may see Jesus in your life. No better time than now. The world needs more of Jesus. Lift Him Up!

DAY 177

MANIFESTING GODLY MEN

"I have manifested Your name to the men whom You have given Me out of the world. They were Yours. You gave them to Me, and they have kept Your Word. Now they have known that all things which You have given Me are from You." –*John 17:6-7*

This deep passage can apply to those involved in men's ministry, and to those parents raising sons to become godly men. We have the responsibility to make the Lord's name real to them; to provide a path of true righteousness that leads surely to Christ. To guide them by the Word to the Word in a manner that increases their desire to know more of Him. Rather than seeking the accumulation of goods that contribute to pride, teach them to seek the Lord. He makes rich and adds no sorrow to it. The enemy seeks to destroy the Seed. We must be conscious of our place to train, lead, and provide godly models of all men. God's principles apply to us all. Godly men manifest godliness, and train other godly men.

WICKED IS NOT GOOD

"When the wicked comes, contempt comes also; and with dishonor comes reproach." *–Proverbs 18:3*

Three Things

1. Bad things come with wickedness
2. It brings contempt and dishonor
3. Reproach soon follows

You live seeking righteousness and holiness now. But avoid any contact with wickedness, even the "small" wicked things acceptable to others. Once you allow the wicked to frequent your presence, they begin to erode your place with God. First, they exhibit contempt, having become familiar with you. Then they disrespect and dishonor you with every opportunity. As it becomes clear that you will accept this position, reproach comes from God and man. This is a fall from grace not worth experiencing. Scripture reminds us to walk worthy of our calling. Avoid wickedness in any form. It is not good for you and will not be good to you.

CHANGE DIRECTION

"For if the firstfruit is holy, the lump is also holy; and if the root is holy, so are the branches." *–Romans 11:16*

Every part of the tree shares the characteristics of that tree. We are joined to the Father as a branch connected to Jesus Christ. The Father is holy, and so is His Son. Scripture states that we are to be holy as He is holy. He would not have commanded that if it were not possible. We must pursue holiness as a core part of our existence on this earth. We seek holiness by seeking God. The closer we get to God, the more we learn of holiness. And what we can learn, we can live. Holiness is not put on like a coat; it is absorbed through practice, understanding, and being exposed to it. You don't "feel" holy, you become holy. Flee from sin, pursue holiness. In both cases, you are running. The difference is the direction.

CORRECT THEM RIGHT

"Do not withhold correction from a child, for if you beat him with a rod, he will not die. You shall beat him with a rod, and deliver his soul from hell." *–Proverbs 23:13-14*

Three Things

1. Correct children who need it
2. Spank them if called for
3. Correction will deliver him from hell

Discipline is necessary to keep order within any household. That correction will keep a child from developing habits that lead to hell. There may be times when correction includes physical punishment to ensure that there is no repeating of the behavior. Such discipline will not kill; but will be remembered. Scripture reminds us that whom God loves, He corrects. All correction and discipline should be given with love. Examine your heart and teach your children rightly. Raise them in the fear and admonition of the Lord. Train and correct, but correct them the right way, to keep them on the right path.

HE ANSWERS YOUR CALL

"Save me, O God, by Your name, and vindicate me by Your strength. Hear my prayer, O God; give ear to the words of my mouth." –*Psalm 54:1-2*

Three Things

1. God saves by His name
2. He vindicates by His strength
3. He hears when we call

We serve a God who is able to save, mighty in battle, and hears our cry. Scripture reminds us that He will never leave us nor forsake us. When we are in danger or in need, He will come to our rescue. One Scripture declares, "Call to Me, and I will answer you, and show you great and mighty things which you do not know." God has no limits. If we believe and trust Him enough, He will save us for eternity, and deliver us right now. Draw close to God, and He will draw close to you! Need Him? He is just a prayer away. Let Him hear your voice. He will be pleased.

SENT TO LABOR

"But when He saw the multitudes, He was moved with compassion for them, because they were weary and scattered, like sheep having no shepherd. Then He said to His disciples, 'The harvest truly is plentiful, but the laborers are few. Therefore pray the Lord of the harvest to send out laborers into His harvest.'" –*Matthew 9:36-38*

The multitudes are in the field, just waiting to hear the Word that will bring them to the safety and protection of the Good Shepherd. We see them wandering in the stores, along the street, and even at work! Yet fear and selfishness keeps us from sharing the Love they need. Believer, have you accepted Christ? If so, then the Holy Spirit resides within your heart. He is the One who draws laborers to the great privilege of sharing the gospel. The miracle is not in the pulpit. The miracle happens when you share the gospel with a lost sheep, and their life is changed. You are a laborer, and He is sending you.

WHAT DO YOU HAVE

"The locusts have no king, yet they all advance in ranks; the spider skillfully grasps with its hands, and it is in kings' palaces." –*Proverbs 30:27-28*

Three Things

1. God gives all creatures abilities
2. Locusts organize to advance
3. Spiders spin webs in kings' palaces

How easy it is to compare your ability and condition with others who seem to be better off. But God has provided the right abilities even for creatures we often overlook. Scripture reminds us that the Lord has given us all things pertaining to life and godliness. We have enough to do what we are called to do. But we have not taken inventory of what we already have. Much of our energy is used in comparing ourselves to others. If we are unique, there can be no comparison. Today, take time to consider your storehouse of blessings, gifts, and abilities. Then set about the task of fully using them for God's glory.

DAY 184

A RIGHTEOUS THRONE

"The Lord has established His throne in heaven, and His kingdom rules over all." –*Psalm 103:19*

Three Things

1. God is Lord over all
2. He has established His throne
3. His throne is in heaven

From the beginning of eternity, God has reigned. He has always been God. Scripture reminds us that His throne is forever and ever. Our minds cannot fully comprehend that, just as we struggle to explain the concept of God manifested as Father, Son, and Holy Spirit. Better that we accept it by faith and strive to live a life that pleases God than to reject it and be rejected when it matters most. He has promised that by accepting Christ we have the power to become sons of God. One day we will be seated in heavenly places to rule and reign with Jesus Christ! Crowns of righteousness come from obedience and faith in Him who sits on the Throne. A righteous Throne.

NO TIME TO JUDGE

"Therefore you are inexcusable, O man, whoever you are who judge, for in whatever you judge another you condemn yourself; for you who judge practice the same things. But we know that the judgment of God is according to truth against those who practice such things."
–Romans 2:1-2

Judgment is reserved for God, for only He knows the truth. We have seen the damage caused when others judge the action of someone else, thinking they know the purpose of actions done. Shame results when the truth is uncovered, and the accusers are found guilty instead. It is good to be aware of potential evil in your midst, but don't presume guilt where there is none. Paul stated that he judges no man, not even himself. Sometimes that is the safest path. Judging is often just an excuse to meddle in the lives of others. Better to clean up your own house. There is more piled up in your closet than you want the world to know. Now is not the time to judge others when there is too much work to do on yourself.

JUST A TEST

"A worthless person, a wicked man, walks with a perverse mouth; he winks with his eyes, he shuffles his feet, he points with his fingers; perversity is in his heart, he devises evil continually, he sows discord." –*Proverbs 6:12-14*

Three Things

1. Worthless wicked people should be avoided
2. They do things to be noticed
3. They devise evil and sow discord

Everyone knows who they are. Their loud, vulgar language and coarse behavior is to make sure they are noticed. But their evil heart makes them dangerous, for they live to cause trouble. But we are not to run from such people. Scripture reminds us that we are not given a spirit of fear, but of power, love and a sound mind. Meet such a person confidently, with love and awareness of their deviousness. Outthink them, outlast them, and out love them. God may have sent them to test you and prepare you for the next assignment. Keep in mind that they're just a test.

AUDIENCE OF ONE

"Praise the Lord! Praise the name of the Lord; Praise Him, O you servants of the Lord! You who stand in the house of the Lord, in the courts of the house of our God, Praise the Lord, for the Lord is good; sing praises to His name, for it is pleasant." *–Psalm 135:1-3*

Three Things

1. Praise the name of the Lord
2. If you serve and stand in His house, praise Him
3. It feels good to sing praises to God

If you are a servant of the Lord, praise Him because you can. It is a privilege to serve God in any capacity. No matter where you stand in the house of the Lord, praise His name. If you serve in areas where no one sees the work you do or serve in the parking lot where you are seen by everyone, sing praises to His name. Scripture reminds us that the Lord looks on the heart. Does He see the joy of the Lord in your heart? Don't worry about who is watching you. He is your only audience. Praise Him!

WALK THROUGH THE WILDERNESS

"Immediately the Spirit drove Him into the wilderness. And He was there in the wilderness forty days, tempted by Satan, and was with the wild beasts; and the angels ministered to Him." –*Mark 1:12-13*

Mark makes it sound so easy, but we understand that this was a grueling period for Jesus. Fasting and praying, keeping the Word sharp in His heart to defend against the enemy. Does this sound like something you are going through? Then rejoice that your faith is being tried. The Lord must test your faith to show you that it is true. He knows your heart but is lighting your path while strengthening your walk. And often, time in the wilderness is the surest way to do so. As you move among the wild beasts of sickness, poverty, lack of resources, and doubt, remember that this time will pass. You will emerge victorious and with a stronger assurance that God can do it for you. He will do it. So, walk. The wilderness cannot outlast your faith.

GENTLE DISCIPLINE

"He who spares his rod hates his son, but he who loves him disciplines him promptly." *–Proverbs 13:24*

Three Things

1. Discipline shows love
2. Correction diverts us from danger
3. Apply discipline quickly to discourage habits

I remember only one spanking my mother gave me. It was deserved, and I remember it. I also never did anything to deserve such correction again. In spite of society's opinion, a rod rightly administered in love can change a child's behavior. But one cannot wait until the behavior is habitual or the child is grown to apply correction. It is too late. Scripture reminds us that whom the Lord loves, He corrects and disciplines. I seek a righteous life because discipline is a more difficult path than one of obedience. And if God disciplines with love, that is a good example for us all. We are to discipline gently, with love.

GOD MAKES IT RIGHT

"Righteous are You, O Lord, and upright are Your judgments. Your testimonies, which You have commanded, are righteous and very faithful." *–Psalm 119:137-138*

Three Things

1. The Lord is righteous
2. His commandments are upright
3. In all He does, He is faithful

We can rely on the Lord, for He is righteous, upright, and faithful in all He declares. Scripture reminds us that the promises of God in Him are yes and amen. There is no wavering or doubt in the Lord. When He judges, it is right. When He promises, it is certain. God never changes. Our perception of Him does. As we mature in our faith, we should let the truth of God's Word guide our steps. That requires that we make a determined choice to be obedient. A life of disobedience prevents us from seeing the righteousness of God. Popular opinion does not make it right. Only God does.

LEND A HAND

"Bear one another's burdens, and so fulfill the law of Christ. For if anyone thinks himself to be something, when he is nothing, he deceives himself." –*Galatians 6:2-3*

Love God wholeheartedly, and love your neighbor as yourself, Christ commanded us. So, when I know that you are struggling with a burden that I can help to carry, why not lend a hand? But if my attitude toward you, or my perception of myself prevents my helping, I must consider my heart. Scripture reminds us not to consider ourselves more highly than we ought to. Let's face it, none of are as good nor as holy as we try to present to the world. Our journey of obedience requires that we pay attention to important elements that will help us to mature in Christ. Here indeed is one of those elements. Humility and love is a foundation for faith. Bring your nose down and place your hands alongside your neighbor's. Many hands make light work. Lend a hand.

DAY 192

THE BATTLE WITHIN

"It is honorable for a man to stop striving, since any fool can start a quarrel." *–Proverbs 20:3*

Three Things

1. A man of peace is honored
2. Refusal to fight marks maturity
3. Any fool can start a quarrel

Much confusion and violence are begun because of misunderstanding, miscommunication or misplaced anger. Scripture reminds us that peacemakers are blessed, for they shall be called Sons of God. It can be surmised that those who work to destroy peace are under the influence of a different parentage. It takes little intelligence to start a quarrel, but great restraint is required to avoid one. Society may seem to cheer the attitude of a brawler, but in reality, people prefer to stay their distance from those who fight without reason. Better to be a person of meekness, having much power, but keeping it under control. Showing love brings true relationships and honor. Win the battle from within, and there will be fewer battles without.

DUSTY RETURN

"As a father pities his children, so the Lord pities those who fear Him. For He knows our frame; He remembers that we are dust." –*Psalm 103:13-14*

Three Things

1. A father has compassion for his children
2. The Lord pities those who fear Him
3. He remembers that we are dust

A true father watches over and has compassion for his children. So does the Lord pity those who fear Him, hearing and obeying Him. Scripture reminds us that God knows even the hairs on our head. He remembers that we are dust. So shall we soon remember that our lives are in the hand of the God who created dust. From a small Word came a great world. In time shall it all dissolve. Ashes to ashes, dust to dust. You shall one day return to the God who formed you. But before you do, leave a footprint of love that others may walk the path leading to that God of creation.

GOOD SEED

"'A sower went out to sow his seed. And as he sowed, some fell by the wayside; and it was trampled down, and the birds of the air devoured it. Some fell on rock; and as soon as it sprang up, it withered away because it lacked moisture. And some fell among the thorns, and the thorns sprang up with it and choked it. But others fell on good ground, sprang up, and yielded a crop a hundredfold.' When He had said these things, He cried, 'He who has ears to hear, let him hear!'"
–Luke 8:5-8

Many hear this parable and nod in agreement with the wisdom it contains. I urge consideration in regard to the seed being sown in your life. Is it indeed good seed, or has the sower added some filler that could become weeds in your mind? Sound doctrine is often not popular nor exciting to hear. Strong truth will not bring loud responses of "Amen, Amen!" But truth of scripture is always pure. It is good seed. Sift the seed, as a good Berean. Look for the seeds of truth in the message before you let it bury itself in the good soil of your heart.

DON'T LOSE HOPE

"Do you see a man wise in his own eyes? There is more hope for a fool than for him." –*Proverbs 26:12*

Three Things

1. Wisdom is recognizable
2. Truth is personal and obvious
3. You cannot teach anyone who refuses to recognize the truth

Someone who has become delusional in their ignorance is in a sad state. For them, truth is no longer important, and they will not be corrected. Too many have reached this state in regard to their sin. Scripture refers to such a person as having been blinded by Satan. We are urged to reach them with the truth of the gospel before their consciences become seared, and they no longer feel the need to repent. Once that has happened, only a miracle can restore life to their soul. Be that source of light for those who cannot see. Point to the One who is light. He is the only hope for the hopeless. Don't lose hope, God can work miracles. He is both light and life.

THIRSTY FOR LIVING WATER

"As the deer pants for the water brooks, so pants my soul for You, O God. My soul thirsts for God, for the living God. When shall I come and appear before God?" –*Psalm 42:1-2*

Three Things

1. My soul pants for God
2. It is an urgent need
3. I long to be in His presence

Only when we mature in faith and have experienced issues of life can we realize how much we need God. Scripture reminds us that without God, we can do nothing. There are times when God will let us try to tackle life armed with our pride and attitudes of self-confidence. When we have failed, He waits for us to turn back to Him. True faith is revealed when we love Him enough to need Him. Then we don't see Him as an accessory. He is life itself. Are you thirsty for life? Then you are dry without His Living Water. Drink deep, and you will never thirst again.

STAND, DON'T FALL

"And he said to Him, 'All these things I will give You if You will fall down and worship me.' Then Jesus said to him, 'Away with you, Satan! For it is written, 'You shall worship the Lord Your God, and Him only you shall serve.'" *–Matthew 4:9-10*

Only Satan would have the nerve to request that Jesus, "fall down and worship" him in return for something that He (Jesus) created. The Lord responded rightly, "…it is written". But that encounter should cause us to wonder how many Christians have fallen down to worship the world and the things that are seen within the world? We pray that we all receive strength to know and to follow the Word of God. But that is difficult in a time of chaos and deception. So, we must hide the Word in our heart and remain vigilant against the wiles of the enemy. When you have done all that you can to deal with the issues you face, then stand in faith that God will sustain you. Whatever you do, don't fall for the deception of the enemy that he can "give" you anything that rightly belongs to Jesus. Neither worship the "treasure" the enemy offers in this world. Instead, store up your treasure in heaven and stand strong.

KNOW THE DIFFERENCE

"Woe to those who call evil good, and good evil; who put darkness for light, and light for darkness; who put bitter for sweet and sweet for bitter. Woe to those who are wise in their own eyes, and prudent in their own sight!" *–Isaiah 5:20-21*

Three Things

1. Truth exists to be known as truth
2. Changing the words do not change reality
3. Tragedy lies ahead for those who attempt to be wise through deception

Some intentionally call evil good and good evil. They live in a way that is contrary to proper ideals, preferring to follow their own roads. Scripture reminds us that there is a way that seems right to a man, but its' end is the way of death. Deception leads surely to sin, which has deadly wages. Better to find truth and follow it to a place of righteousness. Find truth in God's Word. It is where we find wisdom. Know the difference. Satan does.

SPEAK IT AND MEAN IT

"They have bowed down and fallen; but we have risen and stand upright. Save, Lord! May the King answer us when we call." –*Psalm 20:8-9*

Three Things

1. Those who bow before evil will fall
2. Those who stand in integrity will rise
3. The Lord will save us when we call

The darkness of a fallen world needs the light of a people whose God is the Lord. Those who bow before evil finds their chains will drive them to the ground. But those who stand in integrity will be lifted by faith in due time. The Lord will save His people when they call. Scripture reminds us that He will answer when we call to Him and will show us great and mighty things that we do not know. If we are to be salt and light to such a world, we must stand upright. God gives power to stand that we may declare His truth. Do not bow down to opinions, threats, or adversity. A solid foundation is beneath your feet. Speak truth like you mean it.

THE HIGHEST DEGREE

"Now when they saw the boldness of Peter and John, and perceived that they were uneducated and untrained men, they marveled. And they realized that they had been with Jesus." *–Acts 4:13*

Many people judge your effectiveness by your background. Your family, city of your birth, and your job status are all assessed before they hear your words. If you speak from the pulpit, your education obtained from the secular, accredited seminary affects their acceptance of scriptural truth. If you do not have one, you get no respect. Personal opinion over truth has permeated even the church. When others realize that you have been with Jesus, it removes the scales from their eyes. Your delivery of the Word is less important than the Word you deliver. This fact is not confined to those serving in pulpits. Every believer is assigned the task of sharing the gospel. When others ask the source of authority for your words, tell them truthfully, "I have been with Jesus." No degree rises above that.

BANISH THE DARKNESS

"Anxiety in the heart of man causes depression, but a good word makes it glad." –*Proverbs 12:25*

What is in your heart can change how you feel and how you relate to others. When you harbor deep anxiety, there is danger of depression. When there is no hope, our emotional response is to hide in darkness. A good word brings light to our heart, lifting up our soul, and our countenance. Scripture reminds us to hide God's Word in our hearts. The light of His Word floods us with hope. Darkness cannot remain when such light is present. As we bring more of God's Word into our heart, we reflect the light of God's love. Others then see that we are salt and light. No darkness there.

SPEAK HIS WORD

"The mouth of the righteous speaks wisdom, and his tongue talks of justice. The law of his God is in his heart; none of his steps shall slide." –Psalm 37:30-31

Three Things

1. The righteous speak differently
2. They speak wisdom and justice
3. They walk firmly, according to God's Law which is in their heart

The world, accustomed to hearing lies, is uncertain how to deal with the righteous. Speaking wisdom, knowing justice, and being in their presence irritates sinners. Even as society reaps judgment from their ungodly lifestyle, the righteous stand on solid ground. Scripture reminds us to build on the rock, which is Jesus Christ. When we are guided by the Holy Spirit, the truth we speak can change the lives of those who hear. It is a testimony that God has created a newness of life that includes our mouth. Speak His Word.

CONTAGIOUS LOVE

"We then who are strong ought to bear with the scruples of the weak, and not to please ourselves. Let each of us please his neighbor for his good, leading to edification." *–Romans 15:1-2*

When we encounter those who have difficulty deciding what is right, we should be strong examples of righteousness. Not to condemn their lack of understanding, but to help them grow in knowledge. Our strength of faith leads us to a closer walk with the Lord. But those who are following the world lack the assurance of an eternity in heaven. Avoid judging those who are misled. We were all in that group before we accepted Christ. Instead, practice the art of love, knowing that the grace of God can shine through us. An understanding smile from the heart is more effective than an accusing attitude. Be strong enough to love those who are weak. Love is contagious, infect others with it at every opportunity.

A SPECIAL GIFT

"He who has pity on the poor lends to the Lord, and He will pay back what he has given." *–Proverbs 19:17*

Three Things

1. Compassion for the poor is good
2. Giving to the poor is lending to God
3. God always pays back good

Jesus said that the poor will always be with us. It seems that poverty surrounds our life, no matter where we live. Rather than ignoring the poor, we should do what we can to help them. Scripture reminds us that we shall reap what we sow. Sharing God's resources and giving compassion to others are good seed. We never know when our lives may be impacted, and we become the one in need. Time is the most valuable resource we have, so if we take time to love those in need, our lives will be enriched as well. Be a blessing to those who need a blessing. Pray, and God will direct your gift to the right person.

TRUST HIS TIMING

"Do not lift up your horn on high; do not speak with a stiff neck. For exaltation comes neither from the east nor from the west nor from the south. But God is the Judge: He puts down one, and exalts another."
–*Psalm 75:5-7*

Three Things

1. Don't be prideful, calling attention to yourself
2. Exaltation does not come from man
3. God judges, and chooses who is exalted or demoted

Those who "toot their own horn" often find disappointment at the end. We should improve ourselves, work to our giftings and strengths; but don't look to man for exaltation. Scripture reminds us that promotion comes from the Lord. God is a righteous judge, and He exalts one, and demotes another. Each day we live allows us to strengthen our faith in Him. We trust that in due time, He will call us up higher, that we may serve Him better! He has the plan. Trust His Timing!

DAY 206

WHO IS SPEAKING?

"But Elymas the sorcerer (for so his name is translated) withstood them, seeking to turn the proconsul away from the faith. Then Saul, who also is called Paul, filled with the Holy Spirit, looked intently at him and said, "O full of deceit and all fraud, you son of the devil, you enemy of all righteousness, will you not cease perverting the straight ways of the Lord?" –*Acts 13:8-10*

There are some who claim great authority, even spiritual power as they approach you. Remember that not all who profess to represent the Lord are truthful. Satan perverts the truth, and those who follow him take the same path. Test the spirits, beloved, to know whether they are of God. An emotional delivery with a powerful voice is only theater if it is not intended to provide the truth of scripture. Be sober and be vigilant. The devil might be influencing the pulpit. If you hear it, pray for a change of heart. We need truth, not persuasion. Know who is speaking.

A CLEAR PATH

"Whoever digs a pit will fall into it, and he who rolls a stone will have it roll back on him." –*Proverbs 26:27*

Three Things

1. Evil results from evil actions
2. Digging a pit can trap the digger
3. Rolling stones cannot be controlled

Evil is dangerous to those who live with evil intent. The God of Justice warns against sowing that which you do not want returned to you. For those who live in the righteousness of the Lord, scripture assures us that no weapon formed against us shall prosper. Pits, stones being rolled, fiery darts are all deflected by His mighty arm of protection. There will always be battles, and at times we will receive wounds. But if we walk in the path of righteousness, even the shadow of death is fleeting. Walk carefully along the path He lights for us. Soon we will dine at the table He has spread before our enemies. No pitfalls or stumbling blocks. Just blessings and a clear path leading to them.

DAY 208

HE IS GOD

"Forever, O Lord, Your word is settled in heaven. Your faithfulness endures to all generation; You established the earth, and it abides."
–*Psalm 119:89-90*

Three Things

1. What the Lord establishes remains forever
2. His Word is settled in heaven
3. His faithfulness and creation endure

Our Lord is a solid rock, whose very word is established forever in heaven. The earth was established by His Word and abides at His command. He is a faithful God who never changes. Scripture reminds us that He is the same yesterday, today, and forever. We are assured that such will endure to all generations. In a world where attitudes, beliefs, and cultures can change based on personal feelings, it is good to wake up each day to a God who loves us the same. And that will not change like the weather. God will always be God.

KNOW GOD

"Jesus spoke these words, lifted up His eyes to heaven, and said, 'Father, the hour has come. Glorify Your Son, that Your Son also may glorify You, as You have given Him authority over all flesh, that He should give eternal life to as many as You have given Him. And this is eternal life, that they may know You, the only true God, and Jesus Christ whom You have sent.'" –*John 17:1-3*

The season is here to know the Father and Jesus Christ (who was sent by the Father). We celebrate the sacrifice of Jesus and gladly accept the salvation He offers. The gifts are often honored above the Giver and we pridefully declare our exalted position of acceptance into the kingdom. But can we take the time to know the King, in whose kingdom we will reside eternally? Do not become stiff-necked and prideful as you grow prosperous. All you have come from Him. Humble yourself under the mighty hand of God. He gives grace to the humble but resists the proud. Open the Book. It is time to learn of Him.

DAY 210

CUT OFF FROM GOD

"But the wicked will be cut off from the earth, and the unfaithful will be uprooted from it." –*Proverbs 2:22*

Three Things

1. Wickedness leads to isolation
2. God is not pleased with unfaithfulness
3. Unfaithfulness will be uprooted

God does not like sin and wickedness. Such results in His judgment, and ultimately separation from Him. Scripture reminds us that God will remove from His presence those who practice iniquity, those who profess holiness, but have not known Him. God seeks true fellowship with us. He paid a great price to redeem us from the snares of Satan. But sin separates us from God, and only a true relationship, gained through accepting Jesus, will save us. You cannot hold on to the sins of the world and hope to enter heaven. Be faithful to your God and serve only Him. It is lonely in the outer darkness without Him. Don't be cut off from God.

WAIT AND PRAY

"Wait on the Lord, and keep His way, and He shall exalt you to inherit the land: when the wicked are cut off, you shall see it." *–Psalm 37:34*

Three Things

1. Patience and perseverance bring rewards
2. God shall exalt you on high
3. You will witness the wicked falling

Wait on the Lord to bring good things to pass. Let Him set things right. Scripture reminds us that vengeance belongs to the Lord. If we continue the path of righteousness, God notes our diligence. He will exalt us in due time, granting a right inheritance to us. But those who practice wickedness will be cut off. We shall see it. Nevertheless, pray for those who seek your harm. Walk in love, even as you guard your heart. It could be that the grace of God will turn that enemy into a believer. We can only pray.

DRINK DEEP

"And He said to them, 'To you it has been given to know the mysteries of the kingdom of God; but to those who are outside, all things come in parables, so that 'Seeing they may see and not perceive, and hearing they may hear and not understand; lest they should turn, and their sins be forgiven them.'" –*Mark 4:11-12*

When you have truly accepted Christ, the Holy Spirit dwells within you. When you spend time in the Bible, He opens the meaning of scripture. The mystery of the kingdom of God unfolds before you. It is not so for non-believers. No matter how lofty their education, they will not understand until the Spirit of Truth illuminates their mind. If time in God's Word is not like the need for water, there is something wrong. Ask the Lord to fill you with His Holy Spirit. Then open His Word, and drink deeply from His fountain of knowledge.

LIGHT OF TRUTH

"The people who walked in darkness have seen a great light; those who dwell in the land of the shadow of death, upon them a light has shined." –*Isaiah 9:2*

Three Things

1. A change has come to the people
2. Those in darkness have seen a great light
3. Those in shadow now live in light

God did not mean for His people to live in darkness, or the shadow of death. Scripture reminds us that the Lord is the light of the world. Though we walk through the valley of the shadow of death, we must not fear evil! When we are tempted to despair and darkness dims our vision, that is when a great light will shine upon us. The light of hope that comes through faith. With unwavering faith, we can stride boldly into the world that needs the light we have become. Only through Christ – the Light of the World. The True Light of Truth.

BE WASHED

"These things you have done, and I kept silent; you thought I was altogether like you; but I will rebuke you, and set them in order before your eyes." –Psalm 50:21

Three Things

1. God's silence is not acceptance
2. God is not like us
3. His rebuke will set us in order

Man has a short memory and excessive pride. We sin and think that God will discount our actions or that He "knows our heart." Scripture reminds us that God will not always strive with man. When His patience is exhausted, judgment will come. God will rebuke us for our sin and set in order the mess we have made. It would be wise to repent now. Abandon your wicked ways and stand in the cleansing stream of God's forgiveness. Being washed in the Blood of Jesus is the only way to salvation. Be washed or be judged. You choose.

SHARING GOOD NEWS

"For if I preach the gospel, I have nothing to boast of, for necessity is laid upon me; yes, woe is me if I do not preach the gospel! For if I do this willingly, I have a reward; but if against my will, I have been entrusted with a stewardship." –*1 Corinthians 9:16-17*

We have been commanded to go into all the world and make disciples of Jesus. Therefore, we must all, in effect, preach the gospel. It is not a commodity to trade for wealth, nor a production designed to make one famous. It is a profound truth to turn mankind away from sin and back to the Father. It can only be accomplished by accepting the gift of salvation through Jesus Christ. Just fact! Yet fear has stopped many from sharing that truth with others bound for hell. "My people perish for lack of knowledge" is a sobering statement. Know how to share (preach) the gospel. Sharing this is good news indeed!

DAY 216

PATH TO INNER PEACE

"He who is slow to anger is better than the mighty, and He who rules his spirit than he who takes a city." –*Proverbs 16:32*

Three Things

1. Anger is not might
2. Conquering a city is only one strength
3. Controlling anger, and ruling over one's spirit is the true strength

Warriors and strong people make displays of their ability. They seek the adoration of others to validate themselves. Scripture reminds us that meekness indicates true strength. Jesus referred to Himself as "meek and lowly, so such a characteristic must have importance in His eyes. The same One who has all power in His hand demonstrates the power of love. Only through the Holy Spirit can we gain control of our own spirit. To others, that may seem like weakness. But when we are weak, He is strong. And when the situation arises, I would rather God be strong on my behalf. Slow the anger, guide your spirit. Shalom.

"GIMME" GETS IN THE WAY

"You are my God, and I will praise You; You are my God, I will exalt You. Oh, give thanks to the Lord, for He is good! For His mercy endures forever." –*Psalm 118:28-29*

Three Things

1. I will praise and exalt God
2. Give thanks, for He is good
3. His mercy endures forever

With every breath, we should be praising and exalting God. We need no other reason except the fact that He is God! Giving thanks for His goodness is easy. The breath in your body will remind you. But He is not a moody, temperamental God. His mercy endures forever. If the conditions of your life prevent you from praising God, know that there are many with less than you have, yet they find a way to praise God for the little they have. If you are prideful, greedy, or selfish, you cannot see God's blessings. Take the "Gimme" out of your prayers. Replace it with "Thank You Lord for Your Love."

GOOD FRAGRANCE

"Now thanks be to God who always leads us in triumph in Christ, and through us diffuses the fragrance of His knowledge in every place. For we are to God the fragrance of Christ among those who are being saved and among those who are perishing." *–2 Corinthians 2:14-15*

We are representatives of Christ, led by the Holy Spirit, and sent on a mission of mercy to bring the lost back to the Father. God leads us in triumph and has anointed us for the work. Although we do not see it, the labor in God's field results in a fragrance. As we share the knowledge of God, the fragrance of Christ is diffused in every place we labor. The labor is hard, and we often fight the discouragement of slow results. But do not grow weary in well doing. We will reap in due season if we continue in our work. Focus on sharing, studying, and living the Word of God. The fragrance of your labor pleases God.

BE FAITHFUL

"Hear, my son, and be wise; and guide your heart in the way. Do not mix with winebibbers, or with gluttonous eaters of meat; for the drunkard and the glutton will come to poverty, and drowsiness will clothe a man with rags." – *Proverbs 23:19-21*

Three Things

1. Follow the right path to success
2. Avoid drunkards and gluttons
3. Work diligently to avoid poverty

Wisdom of elders are worth hearing and following. Determine in your heart to walk in integrity. Do not spend time with drunkards and gluttons, who seek only to satisfy their flesh. Focus on working diligently as unto the Lord. Become known for being trustworthy and hard working. Using your gifts to serve others and for the glory of God is the mark of a servant of God. Scripture reminds us that he who is faithful in what is least is faithful in much. God will reward us for being faithful. Just keep the right company.

CHOOSE TO TURN

"Let God arise, let His enemies be scattered; let those who hate Him flee before Him. As smoke is driven away, so drive them away; as wax melts before the fire, so let the wicked perish at the presence of God." *–Psalm 68:1-2*

Three Things

1. We need God to be lifted up today
2. Let the enemies of God be defeated
3. Let wickedness perish

Wickedness is popular today, as each man does what is right in his own eyes. We play with evil and tolerate sin. Scripture reminds us that God is a purifying fire. At the appointed time, He will rise up in judgment, and no sin will exist in His presence. Seek the Lord while He may be found. Repent and receive the forgiveness that only He can give. You don't want to continue as an enemy of God, living for the pleasures of sin. A better life awaits those who turn from their wicked ways. Choose wisely.

TIME TO CHANGE

"But you have not so learned Christ, if indeed you have heard Him and have been taught by Him, as the truth is in Jesus: that you put off, concerning your former conduct, the old man which grows corrupt according to the deceitful lusts, and be renewed in the spirit of your mind." –Ephesians 4:20-23

If your behavior remains the same as it was before you professed being a Christian, you have more learning to do. Scripture reminds us to crucify the flesh daily, and to love God with all that we are. When temptation to return to the old patterns of conduct seems to emerge, we must determine to resist. Seeking righteousness will become a habit when we refuse to accept anything less from ourselves. Be aware that voices will arise against your new standard of life. Look to see who protests righteousness. It is certainly not God. Hear His voice only and change your thinking and behavior. The time is now.

DAY 222

SEE THE RIGHT

"For three things the earth is perturbed, yes, for four it cannot bear up: for a servant when he reigns, a fool when he is filled with food, a hateful woman when she is married, and a maid servant who succeeds her mistress." –*Proverbs 30:21-23*

Three Things

1. Some things disturb even nature, and is therefore not right
2. Those who assume authority unworthily
3. Others have character that is toxic

Some things are just not right. Everyone who sees it is aware, and it seems that even the atmosphere around them is wrong. It is most obvious from those who play a role to get what they want, masking their intentions with a smile. Scripture reminds us to be aware of wolves in sheep's clothing. When they are able, they destroy and wound. Protect your flock, beginning with your family and yourself. Pray for discernment but develop the strength to fight. Draw near to God, and He will draw near to you. It is easy to resist the devil when you are in the presence of God. Now that is something that is right.

A JOYFUL SONG

"I will sing of mercy and justice; to You, O Lord, I will sing praises. I will behave wisely in a perfect way. Oh, when will You come to me? I will walk within my house with a perfect heart." *–Psalm 101:1-2*

Three Things

1. We should sing praises to God
2. It is wise to behave in a perfect way
3. We anticipate His return, and it helps us to walk with a perfect heart

When we sing of mercy and justice, we must sing praises to the God of mercy and justice. We become wise when we seek His face. That path of righteousness makes us yearn for His return. That helps us to walk, even in our own house, with a perfect heart. Scripture reminds us that He seeks those whose heart is perfect toward Him. How can singing praise to God lead to a heart that is perfect? Ask the Holy Spirit who lights both our heart and the path we walk on. With joy in your heart – sing! The Father hears and smiles.

NOT LIKE YOU

"Do not be unequally yoked together with unbelievers. For what fellowship has righteousness with lawlessness? And what communion has light with darkness? And what accord has Christ with Belial? Or what part has a believer with an unbeliever?
–2 Corinthians 6:14-15*

Not everyone follows the Lord, seeks God's face, or obeys His Word. When you are committed to a life that honors God, the enemy becomes your enemy. When you follow a crowd bound for destruction, they will drag you down with them. So, it is better for you to avoid being connected to those who seek anything that is not pleasing to God. You are not like them when you are a child of God. It is not a matter of your being "better than" anyone else. We follow One who has no equal. And He is in the process of making us like Him. Don't jump off the Potter's wheel into the mud. Clean is better. Walk with those who understand that fact. They are not like you if they are not seeking God, or when they despise righteousness. Share the truth in love but look for the right ones to travel with.

PRICE TOO HIGH

"So she caught him and kissed him; with an impudent face she said to him: 'I have peace offerings with me; today I have paid my vows. So I came out to meet you, diligently to seek your face. And I have found you.'" –*Proverbs 7:13-15*

Three Things

1. Temptation is bold and straightforward
2. Religious behavior can mask evil desires
3. Sin will seek you out

Church is not always a place of holiness. Those exhibiting the behaviors of righteousness may be initiators of temptation. When the church is dismissed, and opportunity arises, temptation may approach you. Boldly, and with obvious intent, sin will test your faith. Scripture reminds us to flee from temptation. Yielding to lust can lead to death. Maintain your integrity. Sinful pleasure is not worth damnation. Too high a price to pay.

REAL WORSHIP

"Serve the Lord with fear, and rejoice with trembling. Kiss the Son, lest He be angry, and you perish in the way, when His wrath is kindled but a little. Blessed are all those who put their trust in Him." *–Psalm 2:11-12*

Three Things

1. Serve the Lord with fear, rejoice with trembling
2. Be real in your love for Jesus
3. Blessed are those who trust Him

For some, serving the Lord is a show intended to impress others. They rejoice as a competition, an emotional display to make themselves feel good. We are ever before the Lord, scripture reminds us, and He sees the very intentions of our heart. That alone should make us remember His holiness and tremble. Our purpose is to serve Him. Our privilege is to worship Him. Do you dare to bring strange fire to His altar? Be real in your love for Him. Sin can bring His anger. Put your trust in Him and be blessed. This is not a show or a rehearsal. It is time to get real.

SHOW THEM THE WAY

"This I say, therefore, and testify in the Lord, that you should no longer walk as the rest of the Gentiles walk, in the futility of their mind, having their understanding darkened, being alienated from the life of God, because of the blindness of their heart; who, being past feeling, have given themselves over to lewdness, to work all uncleanness with greediness." *–Ephesians 4:17-19*

For some, such an existence is exciting, maybe even profitable. But you have tasted of God's goodness and know the eternal treasure which awaits you. The pleasures of earth cannot compare with the fulfillment of God's promises in heaven. Knowing this, we cannot walk as others, despising holiness and our assignment to spread the gospel. Our meat is to obey the Word of God! Our treasure is to see men saved from sin. Our joy is found in the relentless pursuit of righteousness. By Him, each day we are conformed to a standard set in heaven to be fulfilled on earth. They don't know the Way. Show them.

TAKE THE FAVOR

"Fools mock at sin, but among the upright there is favor." –*Proverbs 14:9*

Three Things

1. Sin must be taken seriously
2. Fools mock at sin
3. The upright receive favor

God has spoken clearly in His Word about sin. He hates sin. Sin destroys everything it touches. Fools mock this fact because they do not believe sin will destroy them. Scripture reminds us that the fool has denied the existence of God in his heart. So, they join the crowds of the willfully deceived, who refuse to repent of their evil ways. Their wages is death. The upright continues the path that pleases God and receives His favor. That favor is not self-promoting, but often is experienced as a small change in circumstances. Just enough to allow the servants of God to accomplish their work. Unheralded, often unnoticed. Their fruit comes from changed lives. Their reward is in heaven. Favor from God has a tremendous impact eternally.

FAITHFULLY SERVING

"My eyes shall be on the faithful of the land, that they may dwell with Me; he who walks in a perfect way, he shall serve Me."
–Psalm 101:6

Three Things

1. God is watching the faithful
2. The faithful may dwell with God
3. Those who walk perfectly shall serve God

The faithful of the land are being watched. Not only by men, but also by God. When you are faithful, you are guided by faith. That allows you to walk in a perfect way. Scripture reminds us to be holy, as God is holy. Walking with God leads to holiness. As a servant of God, you learn to be a servant for God. It is God who perfects us and gives us the heart for His people. You cannot serve God if you cannot serve the people that God loves. There is no course in Bible College or Seminary that prepares us for that. Only a close walk with Jesus humbles us enough to serve God by serving His people. God is watching. Are you faithfully serving?

A COURTEOUS TRADITION

"'For laying aside the commandment of God, you hold the tradition of men – the washing of pitchers and cups, and many other such things you do.' He said to them, 'All too well you reject the commandment of God, that you may keep your tradition.'" *–Mark 7:8-9*

So often we set aside the commandment of God to go into all the world, preach the gospel, and make disciples. We point to others and make excuses to why we should not be the ones. God has even made it easier for us. We don't have to go to other countries; if we step into any local mall, the countries of the world walk past us. We are more prone to talk to others about the problems of the world than to turn the conversation toward the Problem-solver. It is time to change our tradition to one that keeps us in the Lord's presence. If you are constantly walking with Him, it is easy to introduce Him to others. That is simply a tradition of courtesy. Introduce your companion. Is it Jesus?

BE LIKE JESUS

"The soul of the wicked desires evil; his neighbor finds no favor in his eyes." *–Proverbs 21:10*

Three Things

1. Your soul determines your actions
2. When you seek evil, you get evil
3. All around you are affected by your actions

Someone with an evil attitude could be exhibiting what is foremost in their soul. Your soul determines your actions, and how you relate to the world. When you watch carefully, you discover that some people just desire evil. Avoid them. Scripture reminds us that as a person thinks in their heart, so is he. Focus your soul on things that uplift and bring closeness to God. Learn to love, that God may use you wherever He sends you. Should He place you in the company of someone wicked; just observe their actions. It could be that God is giving you an object lesson. He could be saying, "Don't be this way. Be like Jesus!" Now you have the opportunity to put your faith in action. Be like Jesus!

DAY 232

LOOK TO THE HILLS

"Why are you cast down, O my soul? And why are you disquieted within me? Hope in God; for I shall yet praise Him, the help of my countenance and my God." –*Psalm 42:11*

Three Things

1. We should examine our soul in sadness
2. We must hope in God always
3. He alone is the answer forever

When our heart is heavy and our soul wrestles with issues that push us away from God, we should question ourselves. Yet the answer will not be found in any self-help approach. We will find hope only in God. As we search His Word and seek His face, our assurance becomes clear! He alone is God and has set forth a plan to keep us and to strengthen us. Scripture reminds us that we may walk through the valley of the shadow of death without fear. Those times can impact our soul but must not hobble our faith. He is with you, that you may learn to be with Him. Look to the hills; your help is just a prayer away.

FAMILY REUNION

"And let us consider one another in order to stir up love and good works, not forsaking the assembling of ourselves together, as is the manner of some, but exhorting one another, and so much the more as you see the Day approaching." *–Hebrews 10:24-25*

The gathering of family must be a joyous event, a time of sharing what you are together. The family of God, the Body of Christ should be no exception. When we come to a family reunion, we look forward to seeing those we have not seen in a while. We set aside past problems and embrace the future to come. We anticipate the fellowship and food that nourishes, and the love that satisfies our soul. If you attend church as an obligation or to maintain appearances, you miss out on so much. Time with the family of God is practice, preparing you for an eternity together. This is a family reunion for you by God, right here on earth. Don't miss it.

CHASING GOD'S RICHES

"To show partiality is not good, because for a piece of bread a man will transgress. A man with an evil eye hastens after riches, and does not consider that poverty will come upon him." –*Proverbs 28:21-22*

Three Things

1. Both poverty and riches test character
2. Hunger drives transgression
3. Riches encourage foolishness

Many are either running from poverty or running after riches. But our character keeps us from becoming obsessed with either condition. Scripture reminds us that we must learn to be content in whatever state we are in, rich or poor. There is always a risk that temptation will lead us to tragedy. It is wise for us to evaluate ourselves, and not allow our desires to drive our actions toward evil. When we allow the Holy Spirit to direct our life, He will provide the best path for us. Obedience will result in our abiding in the richness of God's love. That is the only riches worth chasing.

TRUSTING HIM

"O Lord my God, in You I put my trust; save me from all those who persecute me." –*Psalm 7:1*

Three Things

1. God indeed is Lord
2. There is none better to trust
3. God will save us from persecution

The world is not your friend. When you strive for righteousness, persecution will result. Scripture reminds us that because the world hated Jesus, it will also hate His followers. Some yield to this resistance by becoming part of the world. But although we are in the world, we are not to be of the world in its' sins. God will indeed save us from persecution if we trust Him. That includes the need to obey Him. The Lord provides clear instructions that will keep us from sin. When we walk the path of righteousness, weapons of persecution may form, but will not prosper. Keep trusting Him, you will not be disappointed.

GO HOME

"And when He got into the boat, he who had been demon-possessed begged Him that he might be with Him. However, Jesus did not permit him, but said to him, "Go home to your friends, and tell them what great things the Lord has done for you, and how He has had compassion on you." –*Mark 5:18-19*

Jesus saved this man, showed love to him, and then sent him back to minister to his friends. The greatest Teacher and Fisher of men demonstrated His work, not just spoke His Word. This miracle of freeing the man from demon possession was a demonstration of the power of Jesus' love. Too often we want power but not the responsibility of love. Hence the ministry assignment from Jesus was for this man to go home to his friends and tell them what he had received. Not just the work of a miracle but the love and compassion. Jesus could have added this man to his staff and used him as proof of His power. But He sent the man to people who would know the truth of his conversion. True ministry happens with people and is not just confined to a pulpit. Minister to the people. Go home and tell them.

ARE YOU READY NOW?

"But God demonstrates His own love towards us, in that while we were still sinners, Christ died for us. Much more then, having now been justified by His blood, we shall be saved from wrath through Him." –*Romans 5:8-9*

I have heard it said that God does not hear the prayer of sinners. But I know that is not true, for He heard the cry of my heart seeking Him when sin threatened my very soul. He not only heard but showed me a way out of darkness, then lit the path on which I was to walk. A path that kept me in His way. I cannot boast of that blessing because it is available to all who need the love of God. My purpose is to tell you that God's love is available. Right now. He has always been there but maybe you weren't ready for a love that perfect. He is waiting to demonstrate how His love can change your life. Eternally. Are you ready now?

A FAMILIAR VOICE

"Give ear, O Lord, to my prayer; and attend to the voice of my supplications. In the day of my trouble I will call upon You, for You will answer me." –*Psalm 86:6-7*

Three Things

1. Hear me Lord, when I call
2. When I am in trouble, I will call
3. I know that You will answer me

We need assurance that the Lord will hear our prayers. So, we must maintain relationship with Him. The more we spend time with the Lord, we realize that He has always heard our prayers. Trouble is always close by. So, when we need to call on Him in time of need, how comforting to know that He will answer. Stay prepared, beloved one, by speaking to God daily. Let Him become used to hearing your voice. He loves to know that you are reaching out to Him. Not from need but because you love Him. Be a familiar voice to His ears.

BETTER WAY

"Do not enter the path of the wicked, and do not walk in the way of evil. Avoid it, do not travel on it; turn away from it and pass on."
–*Proverbs 4:14-15*

Three Things

1. The wicked follow evil paths
2. Do not follow their way
3. Step around evil and move on

There is an abundance of evil temptation evident today. It is difficult not to see the ways of the wicked. Such people have become accepted and even admired in some circles. Do not be deceived into thinking that the way of evil will result in success. You reap what you sow, and evil ways bring God's judgement. Matthew 7:13 states for us to "Enter by the narrow gate, for wide is the gate and broad is the way that leads to destruction, and there are many who go in by it." Don't go in there, even if many have. Choose the better way.

SHINE IN THE DARKNESS

"You are the light of the world. A city that is set on a hill cannot be hidden. Nor do they light a lamp and put it under a basket, but on a lampstand, and it gives light to all who are in the house. Let your light so shine before men, that they may see your good works and glorify your Father in heaven." *–Matthew 5:14-16*

During times of darkness, the world needs light. Even now, there is a cry for more: more joy, more help, more love. All elements that so many have the capacity to provide. Yet they do not realize that there is a responsibility connected to their gifts. There is a reason that you are blessed with unique skills. The question is: What are you doing with those skills? Seek first the kingdom of God, not fame or fortune. When you reveal God's gifts, He will bring all blessings to you. Now is the time to shine. Not for recognition, but for God's glory. Do good works, and let God work through you. Your light must shine in the darkness.

WISE CHOICE

"Wisdom has built her house, she has hewn out her seven pillars; she has slaughtered her meat, she has mixed her wine, she has also furnished her table." –*Proverbs 9:1-2*

Three Things

1. Wisdom is shown through action
2. Wisdom gets results
3. Wisdom satisfies needs

Wisdom is developed through applied acquired knowledge but is demonstrated through results. In this section of scripture, the emphasis is on the word "has". When you seek advice from someone, you want to find a person who has done it. Theories are fine but are not as important as proven action. By the way, if you are considering the fact of eternity, wisdom indicates that experience reigns there as well. Only One has died and returned from that experience. Following Him is wise.

HE IS HERE

"He sent His Word and healed them, and delivered them from their destructions. Oh, that men would give thanks to the Lord for His goodness, and for His wonderful works to the children of men!"
–Psalm 107:20-21

God's Word is sufficient to heal and deliver us from illness and destruction. As we pray for deliverance, we must also give thanks. God is good to the children of men. His merciful works on our behalf deserves a hallelujah. Our God is indeed worthy of all praise. So, when the world closes in and all hope is tested by darkness, stop and sing praises to the God most high. Not to remind Him that you are here, but to remind yourself that He is!

WAIT FOR THE TRUMPET

"Now we have received, not the spirit of the world, but the Spirit who is from God, that we might know the things that have been freely given to us by God." *–1 Corinthians 2:12*

We who have received salvation have also received the Holy Spirit. So, we are reminded that the confusion we see in this world is not of God. Have we not been told that God is not the author of confusion, but of peace? When the spirit of the world urges chaos, we move to peace and self-control. Meekness is not weakness; it is maintaining control until power is released. Although Goliaths taunt us to storm on to the battlefield, just keep collecting stones. Faith will topple every enemy when it is time. The Spirit says wait but stand prepared. The battle trumpet will sound soon.

GOD'S WAYS

"When a man's ways please the Lord, He makes even his enemies to be at peace with him." –*Proverbs 16:7*

Three Things

1. Our ways can please either God or man
2. Pleasing God is better
3. Peace comes from pleasing God

We become known by our ways. Focusing on changing our ways to please man could result in some enemies. It is better to change our ways to please God. Following God leads to righteousness and undeniable benefits. God's Way of righteousness, truth, and love reflects character in all who choose it. Enemies may not like you, but they will recognize the character of God you display in your ways. The ensuing respect they feel from observing your ways will lead to peace. This is the peace that only God can bring. If you want peace, follow God's way.

TRUTH DISPERSES LIES

"Do not keep silent, O God of my praise! For the mouth of the wicked and the mouth of the deceitful have opened against me; they have spoken against me with a lying tongue." –*Psalm 109:1-2*

Three Things

1. God can speak for us
2. The wicked and deceitful speak against you
3. They lie

Times may arise when voices of the wicked and deceitful rise up against you. It seems that they are intent on drowning out the truth. Although the mouths speak loudly, they lie. Even though it may seem hopeless, do not stop hoping. When you lift up a voice of pleading, the Lord will hear your heart. He will not keep silent but will move on behalf of His children. As Joshua 23:10 declares, "…for the Lord your God is He who fights for you, as He promised you." Truth disperses all lies.

YOUR FIRST DISCIPLE

"My son, give attention to my words; incline your ear to my sayings, Do not let them depart from your eyes; keep them in the midst of your heart." –*Proverbs 4:20-21*

Three Things

1. Fathers should teach their sons God's Word
2. Insist that they pay close attention
3. Remind them to study daily and take them to heart

Fathers are a precious gift to their sons. While they are young, fathers must teach their son the truth of God's Word. Scripture reminds us to train them up in the way they should go, so they will not depart from that path when they are old. Hold their attention with the beauty, adventure, and rewards of living according to God's Word. Tell them the story of Jesus, the greatest hero the world has ever known. Assure them that as a child of God, they can become Men of God. Prepare them for the battles ahead by also showing them how a man of God lives. You are their example of how to follow Christ. So, before you go into all the world to make disciples, begin at home with your own son. He is your first disciple.

WHAT YOU NEED

"Rejoice always, pray without ceasing, in everything give thanks; for this is the will of God in Christ Jesus for you." –1 *Thessalonians 5:16-18*

How can we deal with the issues of life that attempt to crush the hope from our spirit? What is the secret of life, and what is God's will for me? Beloved, these questions and others have troubled men since our fall. The answers lie in our willingness to search scripture, believe His Word, and to be obedient in our application of scriptural truth to our life. Belief without action or action without belief leads to a life of frustration. Here is a 3-step ladder to joy in the Lord that continues even in the most persistent world opposition: Rejoice, Pray, and Give Thanks. That is what He wants and what you need.

GUARD YOUR HEART

"Buy the truth and do not sell it, also wisdom and instruction and understanding." *–Proverbs 23:23*

Three Things

1. Truth is precious
2. Acquire truth, do not surrender it
3. Value, wisdom, instruction and understanding also

God is truth. Much of the world regards truth as optional, dependent upon personal position, or non-existent. As long as the God of Truth lives, seek His truth. Once found, purchase it (acquire it), and honor it as precious. Jesus shed His blood that we may know truth and be set free. Don't sell that truth, trade it for deception, lies, or popular doctrine. Secure that precious truth with the safety straps of wisdom, instruction, and understanding. Guard truth as you guard your own heart.

SOUL MAINTENANCE

"Create in me a clean heart, O God, and renew a steadfast spirit within me. Do not cast me away from Your presence, and do not take Your Holy Spirit from me." *–Psalm 51:10-11*

Three Things

1. God restores our heart and spirit
2. Do not push me away, Lord
3. Keep Your Holy Spirit with me

The world can produce darkness, doubt, and anger in our heart if we accept it. We cannot clean such from our heart; only God can. You know when your heart becomes dark and your attitude changes. Don't ignore it. Seek the light of God before the light of your spirit dims. You were designed to be light to the world. That means you must be in the Light of God constantly to reflect His light. When your heart is damaged, He can clean and repair it. Draw near to God and He will draw near to you. Maybe it is time for a soul maintenance session. Open your Bible.

DAY 250

TIME TO WORK

"For which of you, intending to build a tower, does not sit down first and count the cost, whether he has enough to finish it – lest, after he has laid the foundation, and is not able to finish, all who see it begin to mock him, saying, "This man began to build and was not able to finish." –*Luke 14:28-30*

Life requires planning and application to reach an expected end. A life of faith requires obedience. God has already done the planning for your life; you just have to obey His Word, and the leading of His Holy Spirit. Being concerned about the opinions of others is only important when one is focused on building monuments to oneself. But when our goal is to lift up Jesus, He will indeed draw all men unto Himself. Consider the goal that the Lord has placed in your heart. Realize by faith that you have been given more than enough to finish it. The rest is up to you. Will you obey God's plan for you? Let's get to work.

DAY 251

WASH UP

"There is a generation that curses its father, and does not bless its mother. There is a generation that is pure in its own eyes, yet is not washed from its filthiness." –*Proverbs 30:11-12*

Three Things

1. Generations share characteristics
2. One dishonors its parents
3. It is not aware of its filthiness

Culture can taint behavior and destroy respect. We can see the shared behavior of generations that accept it as normal. A generation has arisen that dishonors its parents and has rejected concepts of purity and holiness. We have seen the result, as sin becomes accepted as a way of life. A city, a country, a people that once embraced the principles of God's Word can soon become an enemy of God. Sin blinds and entangles one that seeks its own way. Who can say when sin has been washed away? Only Jesus can. Are you washed in His blood?

GOD IS STILL HERE

"For the Lord will not cast off His people, nor will He forsake His inheritance. But judgment will return to righteousness, and all the upright in heart will follow it." –*Psalm 94:14-15*

Three Things

1. The Lord will not abandon us
2. Good judgment leads to righteousness
3. The upright will follow that judgment

At times, it seems that judgment has left the world, and the Lord has abandoned us. But faith assures us that God has not left us to the mercy of the evil that grows more apparent. He is our God, and we are His people. We are also His inheritance. As for the bad judgment that has become epidemic, this too shall pass. Judgment will return to righteousness, which is the normal status for God's people. The upright in heart will lead the way back to righteousness. Get your heart right. God is still in charge.

ARE YOU A WATCHMAN?

"I have set watchmen on your walls, O Jerusalem; they shall never hold their peace day or night. You who make mention of the Lord, do not keep silent." –*Isaiah 62:6*

This is still true today. God has placed in the heart of His people the responsibility to watch over those who sleep, that they may be protected from danger. The growth of spiritual attacks has made this responsibility more urgent. Too often, God's people have been silent in the face of deception and tyranny. Do not keep silent. What to speak? God's complete Word of Truth. Not just those scriptures that align with our preferences, but those that bring us back in alignment with righteousness. Scripture reminds us to speak the truth in love. So, when you speak, do so as a messenger of God's Word, not your own opinion. If you are not such a watchman, make way for those who are.

SEEK BETTER

"With her enticing speech she caused him to yield, with her flattering lips she seduced him. Immediately he went after her, as an ox goes to the slaughter, or as a fool to the correction of the stocks." –*Proverbs 7:21-22*

Three Things

1. Enticing speech is attractive
2. Flattery can be seductive
3. Walking into sin is deadly

What we see and the words we hear can overwhelm our better judgment. Satan still uses the lust of the flesh, the lust of the eyes, and the pride of life (1 John 2:16) to kill, steal, and to destroy. If you have decided to follow Jesus, you are a prime target. Temptation is on every hand. Just remember the words of wise minds – "Everything that looks good to you is not always good for you!" If it seems too good to be true, don't trust the set up. Walk past the words and the smiles, seek better.

JESUS SAVES

"For You have delivered my soul from death. Have You not kept my feet from falling, that I may walk before God in the light of the living?" –Psalm 56:13

Three Things

1. The Lord delivered my soul from death
2. He kept my feet from falling
3. I can walk before God in the light of the living

Without the truth of Jesus Christ, our soul and body will turn toward evil. That is where death lies. But the righteousness of God keeps our feet from falling into the pit of temptation. As we walk in the Light, as He is in the Light, we can truly have fellowship with other believers. Only God can deliver us from death and lead us to eternal life. Trust God to fulfill His promises. Shine your light in the darkness that others may accept the truth you now know.

SETTLED

"But may the God of all grace, who called us to His eternal glory by Christ Jesus, after you have suffered a while, perfect, establish, strengthen, and settle you." –*1 Peter 5:10*

I know that part that says, "after you have suffered a while" makes us wonder how long that is. Take heart in the truth that our light afflictions are working for us. God has allowed them to perfect, establish, strengthen, and settle us. I used to hear the older saints say, "You can't have a testimony without a test." That has been a truth to help us endure the molding process that God has prepared for us. Don't compare your situation with others. If they happen to appear strong and unconcerned despite the storms, maybe they have learned to endure. Truthfully, storms are God's recognition that you are mature enough to handle it. Settle in. It will blow over soon. And then you will appear settled to others who have not yet experienced all that you have.

GOOD FEAR

"In the fear of the Lord there is strong confidence, and His children will have a place of refuge. The fear of the Lord is a fountain of life, to turn one away from the snares of death." –*Proverbs 14:26-27*

Three Things

1. Fear of the Lord brings confidence
2. God's children have a refuge
3. Fear of the Lord is a fountain of life

It is good to have a fear of the Lord in this world. Many do not respect themselves, others, or the Lord. When calamity strikes, where can they run for safety? The fear of the Lord draws God's children to the path of righteousness, away from the snare of sin that brings death. They have a place of refuge and hope for tomorrow. Believers have strong confidence in the promises of the Lord, for He cannot lie. Fear God, serve Him, and know the joy of His salvation.

LET YOUR ANGELS REST

"For He shall give His angels charge over you, to keep you in all your ways. In their hands they shall bear you up, lest you dash your foot against a stone." –*Psalm 91:11-12*

Three Things

1. He assigns angels to protect you
2. They do so in all you do
3. To protect you from danger

How precious you are to God, that He will assign His angels to watch over you. How encouraging to know that regardless of the obvious dangers that arise on every hand, the hands of those angels will lift you up. So how are we to respond to that knowledge? Jesus had the answer: do not tempt the Lord your God (Matthew 4:7). The Holy Spirit within you will provide wisdom as surely as the angels provide protection. Listen to Him and avoid the paths of darkness. Don't rush into danger, your angels have enough work to do already. Let them rest awhile.

CHOOSE THE PROMISE

"He did not waver at the promise of God through unbelief, but was strengthened in faith, giving glory to God, and being fully convinced that what He had promised, He was also able to perform."
–*Romans 4:20-21*

It sounds too good to be true when we read or hear those scripture promises that assure us that God will be with us and take care of our needs. Daily we hear the promises of men, who lie as a matter of course. How can we believe the God who created even these men? Through unwavering faith. God's promises are eternal, and based on His character, which is perfect and holy. No comparison. Now comes the hardest part of your work. Will you believe? Despite the chaos and pain in your life, will you let it strengthen your faith? Yes, it is your choice. So, choose this day whom you will serve. His promises for you await your decision.

GUARD YOUR MOUTH

"Whoever guards his mouth and tongue keeps his soul from troubles." –*Proverbs 21:23*

Three Things

1. What you say and eat can change your life
2. We should consider what goes in and what comes out of our mouth
3. Trouble comes from carelessness

Our mouth performs a vital function for life: it receives food for our body and provides communication for understanding. We are reminded that we should guard our mouth and tongue to keep our soul from troubles. Too much of a good thing going in can lead to future medical problems. The wrong words coming out can destroy a treasured relationship. Yes, guard this valuable part of the body, as it can contribute greatly to your joy. When you use it to glorify God and to share the truth of the gospel, everyone is blessed by the hearing of it. Keep your mouth under control and use it sparingly and wisely.

RAISE A PRAISE

"I will praise You, O Lord, among the peoples; I will sing to You among the nations. For Your mercy reaches unto the heavens, and Your truth unto the clouds." –*Psalm 57:9-10*

Three Things

1. I will praise You among all people
2. My song will rise from the nations
3. Your truth and mercy are above all

The statement "When I think about the goodness of the Lord…" is enough to start any believer into fits of praise. Some of us have not gotten so righteous that we have forgotten what God did to set us right. His truth and mercy are far beyond my understanding. Some of us were so lost that only the Lord could have found us. So, there is no right place or time to praise Him, or to lift up a song of thanksgiving. Just remembering that He first loved you and has you foremost on His mind should spark a praise. So, give me a reason to raise my hands and to raise a praise. Be careful, it won't take much!

HARD WORK

"Now he who plants and he who waters are one, and each one will receive his own reward according to his own labor." *–1 Corinthians 3:8*

We have sometimes seen a type of spiritual civil war within the church in which the work is defined by the office held. How can it be that the bishop of several churches is held in higher regard than the street Pastor who possess no building at all, yet brings faith and solace to some who would not be welcomed into a church building? Ephesians 4 informs us that the leaders that are placed into service for God are gifts from God. These are to train up the saints for the work of ministry. That work includes both planting and watering. There is enough work for everyone, and less time than we think. The harvest is plentiful, but workers are few. Come into the field with an intention to do the work you have been called to do, without criticizing the work of another servant. Put on your gloves. This work is hard!

SMELL THE ROSES LATER

"He who tills his land will have plenty of bread, but he who follows frivolity will have poverty enough!" *–Proverbs 28:19*

Three Things

1. Work produces results
2. Working your land brings riches
3. Chasing fun leads to poverty

What others have is for them. When one works the treasure that God has already provided, the result is more satisfying. Diligent work in your own field, business, or home will bring results for you. Choosing to chase after fun, at the expense of working, will bring poverty. God expects us to bring profit from our life – He calls it fruit. This might be a good time to sharpen the skills that God has given you. The more you serve others, the greater the return. Open the shop door, it is time to be about your Father's business. The roses can wait.

DAY 264

OBEDIENCE IS BETTER

"Your hands have made me and fashioned me; give me understanding, that I may learn Your commandments." *–Psalm 119:33*

Three Things

1. You made me
2. You fashioned my life
3. Help me to understand your Word

God creates excellence for His purpose. For those that seek to live in obedience, He fashions the path that strengthens His children. Although we see the circumstances in which God has built our lives, we may find it difficult to understand them. For some, the element of understanding helps them to learn the core commandments of God. For others, the fact that God said it is enough. By faith we walk and trust that understanding will follow eventually. We learn to follow God's Word by living in it. Scripture reminds us that obedience is better than sacrifice. If you can understand that, you are on the way to obeying His commandments.

PRICELESS SOUL

"For what profit is it to a man if he gains the whole world, and loses his own soul? Or what will a man give in exchange for his soul?"
–Matthew 16:26

If only relief could come from the pressure of this world. Some have followed the lead of popularity and closed their eyes of conscience. Financial profit, conspicuous comfort, and joining the crowd to find acceptance should ease the feeling of wrongdoing. But it does not. Short term profit cannot compensate for the deadening of your soul that results from doing wrong. When you truly have accepted Christ, His Holy Spirit will gently guide you. If you ignore His voice, your soul will suffer. You may gain some finances, or even some acceptance by man, but you will soon feel empty inside. Do not let this world destroy your soul. You will need it later.

CHOOSE THE SHINING PATH

"But the path of the just is like the shining sun, that shines ever brighter unto the perfect day." –*Proverbs 4:18*

Three Things

1. The righteous follow a specific path
2. That path shine like the sun
3. It just gets better, leading to perfect

For some, life seems to be gloomy and dark. The unjust seem to follow such a path. But the just seek the path of righteousness. Why does Jesus light our paths? He does not want us falling. As we go further along the path, we find that it leads to Jesus. No wonder it gets brighter. As we walk, we leave our burdens, so it also becomes easier. We have the choice to travel a path of darkness or set our feet on the lighted path. I know which path I choose. But if you choose the other path – watch carefully that you do not stumble.

PROTECTED IN MY WORK

"You have hedged me behind and before, and laid Your hand upon me. Such knowledge is too wonderful for me; it is high, I cannot attain it." –*Psalm 139:5-6*

Three Things

1. You protect me from all directions
2. You have ordained and anointed me
3. I cannot understand it all

After danger has passed and the attack has been destroyed, only then do I recognize the protection of the Lord. I am hedged about, to protect me from fatal blows. I often consider that God has ordained me for work I do for Him. When I attempt to gain for myself, I err. When I advance for the kingdom, only then am I His Ambassador. I will never attain sufficient knowledge to understand that. So, I will simply accept the truth of His Word and step out into the work! I have decided to follow Jesus. No turning back, no turning back. As I serve Him, He is my shield.

GLORY WORKING

"For our light affliction, which is but for a moment, is working for us a far more exceeding and eternal weight of glory." *–2 Corinthians 4:17*

Sometimes the inner thoughts fight the reality of our faith. Small problems loom larger as we ponder them, and we can be tempted to abandon hope. It is then that we should remember. Remember how far He has carried us and how often He has blessed us. We can never exhaust His love or find a false promise in His Word. Why then should we flinch at the light afflictions we now face? Can the false roar of Satan stand before the Lion of Judah? Many have stunted their own spiritual maturity by running from challenges they were built to overcome. Don't cower in darkness. Come into His light. Even your light afflictions are working for you. The best is yet to come. That is glory working.

WISE USE OF SEED

"There is one who scatters, yet increases more; and there is one who withholds more than is right, but it leads to poverty." –*Proverbs 11:24*

Three Things

1. Giving impacts your wealth
2. One who gives to many can be blessed
3. Another who withholds can become poor

Your wealth does not belong to you, but the way you manage it can reveal your character. One realizes that God's money can change the lives of others, and shares widely, yet wisely. Such loving character is soon recognized by God and man. More blessings follow such a one. Another retains selfishly, trying to keep more for himself. Such behavior amounts to burying the one talent God has given to him. His refusal leads to rejection and sometimes to poverty. Take wisdom from God's example, "For God so loved the world that He gave....". Open your hands to give as well as to receive. Giving is a wise use of your seed.

BLESSED WONDER

"I have become as a wonder to many, but You are my strong refuge. Let my mouth be filled with Your praise and with Your glory all the day." *–Psalm 71:7-8*

Three Things

1. Many wonder how I have been blessed
2. My protection and safety is You
3. It is easy to praise You constantly

They remember who I used to be and try to remind me of my old behavior. They wonder how such a change could have occurred. My only answer is simply: God is my refuge. When I trust in the Lord and rest in His arms, He changes my heart. As I consider the fact of His blessings to me, I am continually filled with praise. This is not a brag, just fact. If you have accepted Christ, you also are blessed. And if you remember who you were, maybe you are among the group wondering; Who am I that God should love me so? I am a blessed wonder.

GOOD TREASURE

"A good man out of the good treasure of his heart brings forth good things, and an evil man out of the evil treasure brings forth evil things. But I say to you that for every idle word men may speak, they will give account of it in the day of judgment. For by your words you will be justified, and by your words you will be condemned."
–Matthew 12:35-37

Speaking from the heart can be either good or bad, depending on what is in the heart. You cannot just say what you feel and think it is over. Your words have consequences. The person who receives your words could be damaged or change their perception of you. They could rightly ask how such words could come from a self-described Christian. Listen to what you say before the words come from your lips. Let the Holy Spirit filter your communication. If evil things come from your heart, it is time for a Holy Spirit cleansing. Look closely at your heart. Is there good treasure in there?

SAY IT WELL

"A man's stomach shall be satisfied from the fruit of his mouth; from the produce of his lips he shall be filled." *–Proverbs 18:20*

Three Things

1. We need to eat in order to live
2. Our words attract good things
3. Profit can come from good words

What we say is a result of our determination to communicate what we feel. When we feel confident in ourselves and respect for others, our words will reflect that. Those with the ability to reward us, nurture, or support our goals will rightly trust us if our words are right. Good words, backed by integrity of heart and diligent action, brings wealth. The fruit of our mouth will be trust, which will generate prosperity. Are you hungry? Speak right things to the right people. Begin with yourself.

WORK IN PROGRESS

"The Lord will perfect that which concerns me; Your mercy, O Lord, endures forever; do not forsake the works of Your hands."
–Psalm 138:8

Three Things

1. The Lord will complete what I need
2. God's mercy endures forever
3. He will not forsake His creations

I am assured that the Lord will complete the work of providing what I need in order to finish the work He has given me. He knows what concerns me and will answer that need, often before I ask. His abundant mercy is always with me, enduring forever. I am His child, the work of His hands. He has never forsaken me before, nor will He ever do so. I will lift up my voice daily, praising Him with thanksgiving. I will live in victory because I know the God who truly is God. If you look at my faults and doubt what I say, just know that He is working on me, and on my behalf. I am a work in progress.

DESTINED TO OVERCOME

"For whatever is born of God overcomes the world. And this is the victory that has overcome the world – our faith." –*1 John 5:4*

The world is a dark place for those without the light of the world. Having the light that is Jesus encourages us to resist the devil, and to drive against the circumstances we face. Scripture declares that we overcome by the blood of the Lamb and the word of our testimony, which builds our faith so we can continue to overcome. Isn't it interesting that overcoming adds faith, and faith leads to overcoming? As you read this, consider that your world is the world. You are built to overcome. If it stands between you and God's best for you – it can be overcome. Maybe this obstacle is just a part of the faith-building plan God designed just for you. There is only one way to find out. Overcome it!

RIGHTEOUS RISE

"Do not lie in wait, O wicked man, against the dwelling of the righteous; do not plunder his resting place; for a righteous man may fall seven times and rise again, but the wicked shall fall by calamity."
–*Proverbs 24:15-16*

Three Things

1. Wicked men can plan to destroy the righteous
2. Righteous may be cast down repeatedly, but will rise again
3. Wicked shall fall by calamity

There are wicked people who wait for opportunity to destroy the dwelling, career, or testimony of those seeking righteousness. These efforts may have some results, as they target or hinder, or attempt to cast down the righteous. Yet those seeking righteousness refuse to stay down. They rise, again and again. It may be after a period of recovery or in another location, but they do rise. The wicked will reap what they sow and will fall by calamity. But they will not rise again. Be steadfast, immovable, always abounding in the work of the Lord. He will lift you up.

LIGHT IN DARKNESS

"O Lord, our Lord, how excellent is Your name in all the earth, Who have set Your glory above the heavens!" –*Psalm 8:1*

Three Things

1. You are Lord of all
2. Your name is excellent to all the earth
3. Your glory is set above the heavens

How privileged I am to claim You as my Lord. Yet there is room enough for all mankind to know You as our Lord. For those who know You, even Your name is excellence! We are filled with love and wonder at the mention of Your name. For those who do not yet know you, their soul bows down under the magnificence of Your glory, reflected far above the heavens. That is why I speak Your name before those blinded by darkness. Only the light of Your Word can dispel the darkness of sin and shame. Scripture reminds us that You honor Your Word even above Your name, so shall I hold both in my heart to light the way.

GOOD THOUGHTS

"For I know the thoughts that I think toward you, says the Lord, thoughts of peace and not of evil, to give you a future and a hope."
–Jeremiah 29:11

We often wonder why we were born, why certain events happen in our lives, and where our lives will lead us. Spending too much time wondering can impede our progress to the future. God already knows, even if He has not shared it with us. God is thinking the best for us. Peace, a future, and ultimately eternal life with Him. If we trust Him and seek His face, we will spend less time dealing with doubt. The Lord has given us hope so that we will yearn for the future He has already prepared for us. It takes faith to believe that He is and will provide. So even though you don't know yet, God does. And that is enough. When God thinks good thoughts toward you, good things happen.

HEAR WISDOM CRY

"Wisdom calls aloud outside; she raises her voice in the open squares. She cries out in the chief concourses, at the opening of the gates in the city she speaks her words." *–Proverbs 1:20-21*

Three Things

1. Wisdom calls aloud publicly
2. She can be heard in the streets
3. Wisdom speaks words

In every college, school, and church, many search for wisdom. They assume wisdom comes with age, that others have found wisdom and will share it. If nothing else, surely it can be bought for a price, by those who can afford it! How comforting to know that wisdom speaks outside. In the streets, and within the gates of the city, she speaks her words. But those words can only be heard when we listen, and do not let our inner voice of disbelief and selfishness drown her out. Listen and be wise. Hear the cry of wisdom now.

WONDERFUL GOD

"Oh, give thanks to the Lord, for He is good! For His mercy endures forever. Oh, give thanks to the God of gods! For His mercy endures forever. Oh, give thanks to the Lord of lords! For His mercy endures forever." –*Psalm 136:1-3*

Three Things

1. We have many reasons to give thanks to the Lord
2. He is Lord, God of gods, and Lord of lords
3. He is good, and His mercy endures forever

Our God is worthy of all praise. We should give thanks to Him, for there is none above Him, or like Him. Lord of lords, God of gods, no title can describe Him totally. We bathe in His love, for He is good, and His mercy endures forever. When you hurt, His mercy is there. When you neglect Him until you're in need, His mercy endures. Even when your anger flings words of disrespect in His face, His mercy endures forever. What a wonderful God! Let everyone give thanks for His mercy that endures forever.

AS A CHILD

"But Jesus called them to Him and said, 'Let the little children come to Me, and do not forbid them; for of such is the kingdom of God.' Assuredly, I say to you, whoever does not receive the kingdom of God as a little child will by no means enter it." *–Luke 18:16-17*

When we were first told of Jesus, and accepted His gift of salvation, we trusted His Word. Our hearts were open, believing, and loving. Time and wrong training have taught some to distrust the Word and follow the opinions of popular men. The result has been confusion, anger, and a falling away from truth. Romans 14 reminds us that "…the kingdom of God is not eating and drinking, but righteousness, and peace, and joy in the Holy Spirit." We would be wise to receive those elements as a child: open heart, believing, and loving. We might just find that the kingdom of God is here within our spirit. We just have to push past the "maturity" that blocks our path. Run to Jesus. He waits patiently for those with a childlike spirit.

CHOOSE WISDOM

"I love those who love me, and those who seek me diligently will find me. Riches and honor are with me, enduring riches and righteousness." –*Proverbs 8:17-18*

Three Things

1. Wisdom can be loved, and will love you back
2. Seek wisdom diligently to find her
3. Great rewards will follow when you love wisdom

An occasional relationship with wisdom is not enough. Seeking wisdom diligently will result in a love for wisdom. You will find that righteousness is gained, honor is received, and enduring riches are granted. Seeking wisdom is a life sustaining element with unmeasurable returns. Scripture declares that the fear of the Lord is the beginning of wisdom. It will lead to a life of blessings that can be eternal. When you seek wisdom, you will find the Lord. It is up to you. Choose life, choose wisdom, and choose Jesus.

YOUR DESTINY

"Lord, my heart is not haughty, nor my eyes lofty. Neither do I concern myself with great matters, nor with things too profound for me." –*Psalm 131:1*

Three Things

1. I am not prideful or haughty
2. Great matters do not concern me
3. Profound things do not entrap me

I stay within the life God has given me. I refuse to let my gifts and blessings poison my heart against others. I am simply a child of God with gifted resources to do God's work. Since I am not assigned to wrestle with great issues, I let others do so. Deep and profound things have challenged many noble minds, but that is not my calling. Life's road is filled with many challenges prepared for you. If you are built to confront them, that action will strengthen you. But do not step from the road or take your eyes from the goal God has given you. Accomplish your destiny.

CHECK YOUR SEAL

"Nevertheless the solid foundation of God stands, having this seal: 'The Lord knows those who are His,' and, 'Let everyone who names the name of Christ depart from iniquity.'" *–2 Timothy 2:19*

Regardless of the state of the world, or the lack of faith displayed during times of stress – God has set a solid foundation. That foundation is Jesus, the cornerstone upon which His church is built. To ensure the future for believers, He sealed us with the Holy Spirit as an earnest for what is to come. Standing on the solid foundation, we have the seal (assurance) that the Lord knows that you are His. If you are saved, you are His. But let each one examine himself, to see whether or not he is truly in the faith. If you name the name of Christ, you should have no problem departing from iniquity. A work of obedience and love, not of compulsion. Jesus will forgive every sin, when you confess them. Decide if your faith is words alone, or in obedience to the Word alone. Check your seal.

GET GOOD COUNSEL

"Without counsel, plans go awry, but in the multitude of counselors they are established." –*Proverbs 15:22*

Three Things

1. Counselors are important
2. Without them, plans unravel
3. With enough counselors, plans are established

Ideas and plans flow through the mind of many people. Often, even good plans are lost due to neglect or failure to prepare and implement them. Finding and listening to good counselors helps bring plans to fruition. Without wise counselors, many struggle to make their plans work. Often those plans fail. But the wise person finds counselors with knowledge and expertise. He or she listens to the advice of these trusted people, and they realize success in their plans. In seeking good counsel, consider three facts:
1. Jesus is the answer (to everything)
2. God has a plan for your life
3. Your gifts are given for His glory

If you don't know something, it is best to ask someone who does know – a good counselor.

THROUGH IT ALL

"I will bless the Lord at all times; His praise shall continually be in my mouth." –*Psalm 34:1*

Three Things

1. I have decided to bless the Lord
2. Circumstances will not change this decision
3. My words will offer praise continually

My decisions shape my approach to life and how I express my faith. I have decided to follow Jesus and to believe the truth of scriptures. I have decided to seek righteousness and to obey the commandments of Jesus. I have decided to bless the Lord through speaking my love for Him while showing love to others. These decisions and others that mark me as a child of God, are my reasonable service. I focus my eyes on Him and bless Him with my words as well as my actions. It cannot be a time-limited display but must endure. One old song describes my attitude:

> "Through it all, through it all, I've learned to trust in Jesus, I've learned to trust in God. No matter the resistance, I will persevere through it all."

UNTOUCHABLE

"The Lord shall preserve you from all evil; He shall preserve your soul. The Lord shall preserve your going out and your coming in from this time forth, and even forevermore." –*Psalm 121:7-8*

Three Things

1. The Lord preserves you
2. He protects you from evil, and keeps your soul
3. He will preserve you as you travel

Preserve, protect and present. Strong words representing a strong God. When you serve God, hold unwavering faith in Him, and honor Him, you will be preserved. No danger will befall you or your house. Angels will keep you from dashing your foot against a stone, scripture declares. Blessings will flood your soul and keep your mind stayed on Jesus. When you have run your course, He will present you faultless before the presence of His glory. You are blessed, preserved, and protected. What can man do to you?

BETTER NUTRITION

"""Blessed are those who hunger and thirst for righteousness, for they shall be filled." –*Matthew 5:6*

So often we are tempted by the world to seek after our own pleasure. Advertisements tell us what we should want and direct us to where we should go to get it. Greed, selfishness, and power are lifted up as the best approach to life's happiness. But Jesus said that true happiness (blessings) is found as we hunger and thirst for righteousness. When that becomes as essential as food and water, we will be filled. Scripture declares that He has filled the hungry with good things. Righteousness is one of those good things. God will not withhold any good thing from His children. Turn away from the junk food the world offers through empty promises. Seek the spiritual nourishment of righteousness. It is good for you.

I HAVE LEARNED

"Not that I speak in regard to need, for I have learned in whatever state I am, to be content: I know how to be abased, and I know how to abound. Everywhere and in all things I have learned both to be full and to be hungry, both to abound and to suffer need. I can do all things through Christ who strengthens me." *–Philippians 4:11-13*

Highs and lows, joy, and pain - all events that come with life. If you are breathing, you will experience them all. I have learned that all things change, and no challenge lasts forever! So, we must remember yesterday, enjoy today, and hope for tomorrow. God knows who you are. He built you for this journey and has planned the road ahead. It may seem difficult at times, but along the way you will strengthen your faith. Mature faith is not blown about by winds of adversity. Walk by faith through each day, knowing that it will pass. Smile when you endure it, and simply say, "I have learned."

HEED HIS DIRECTION

"A man's heart plans his way, but the Lord directs his steps."
–*Proverbs 16:9*

Three Things

1. Direction is needed to reach a goal
2. A man's heart plans his way
3. God directs our steps

If you have lived long enough, you can look back over your life and see the places where the Lord directed your steps. There are also the places where our foolishness planned us into problems. Can you rejoice with me for maturity and wisdom to hear God's direction? Pray for the youth of today, for there are more roads available now to lead them astray. Maybe that is why God has built us to walk slower as we age, that we might give a word of wisdom to those rushing by. If they heed the words, they won't need help to get out of the ditch ahead. Walk steadily, step surely, and heed God's direction. He will never steer you wrong.

SPEAK NO EVIL

"Keep your tongue from evil, and your lips from speaking deceit. Depart from evil and do good; seek peace and pursue it."
–Psalm 34:13-14

Three Things

1. Don't speak evil or deceit
2. Do good, not evil
3. Seek peace in your life

When you speak evil or become a party to deceit, you are drawn to danger. Many who thrive on evil pursuits lie in wait for the innocent or uninformed. When you speak evil, some will decide that you are evil. It is better to do good and avoid all evil. Associate with those who do good and, live in peace. Set your boundaries, beloved, to keep influences of evil away from you. We are to be wise in our lifestyle and known by our love. Speak right, live righteously.

RIGHT FAITH

"So Jesus answered and said to them, 'Have faith in God.'"
–Mark 11:22

As we live, we hear the words "Have faith" and we run with it. Through the storms, we struggle to have faith. After getting nowhere, we hear from another source, "Have faith in ___". So, we change the position of our oars, pulling hard to have faith in our knowledge, our education, our wealth, our popularity. Yet we seem to get nowhere, and there is a growing frustration. It seems that everyone has a "word" that we are advised to receive and heed. Once Jesus enters our heart, He has a clear command – "Have faith in God." Now our path is clear, our progress accelerated by the strength of Truth. When we have faith in God, we align our actions with the direction of the Lord of lords. When His heart becomes our heart, nothing is impossible. Listen respectfully to the words of man, but obey the Word sent by God. It will give you the right faith.

RICHES AWAIT

"By humility and the fear of the Lord are riches and honor and life."
–*Proverbs 22:4*

Three Things

1. God honors certain characteristics
2. Humility and the fear of the Lord are key
3. He rewards with riches, honor, and life

Scripture states, "God resists the proud but gives grace to the humble." The prideful struggle with the idea of humility and consequently hold little fear of the Lord. The world lifts up the "winners" and honors those who win at any cost. Such selfishness is counter to Jesus' statement that the first shall be last and the last first. His point was that serving is a virtue for His disciples. That continues to be true today. Jesus came to serve and to die for those who did not deserve such grace. He unselfishly left us with the keys to the kingdom: love, obedience, seeking first the kingdom of God, etc. But wait, you already know all this. If not, be humble enough to admit it, and obedient enough to learn. Riches await you.

BATTLE READY

"Blessed be the Lord my Rock, who trains my hands for war, and my fingers for battle." –*Psalm 144:1*

Three Things

1. Bless the Lord my Rock
2. He trains me for war
3. He prepares me for battle

The Lord of all creation is the Rock who stands for me. He is the One who trains me for the war against evil in all its forms. He strengthens me to stand against that which threatens the weak and the innocent. We wrestle not against flesh and blood, so He trains me for the spiritual battle that is around me and within me. My armor may not be visible, but the enemy recognizes that warriors for God are trained by God. My life is a battle already won. I must occupy the ground that Christ won for me. I stand with warriors of faith, not warriors for show. Which are you? The next battle will reveal the truth to you and reveal those who need your strength. Hold fast to your sword – the enemy lurks near.

DAY 294

IF YOU WILL

"Ask, and it will be given to you; seek, and you will find; knock, and it will be opened to you. For everyone who asks receives, and he who seeks finds, and to him who knocks it will be opened."
–*Matthew 7:7-8*

Action will be followed by response. Jesus is confirming an eternal equation of "If…..then". If you do certain things, then you will experience a response. This is an intelligent teaching from an intelligent God, designed to make His people more intelligent in the Way. Wishing, hoping, and dreaming are passive responses to present difficulties. Demanding, declaring, and railing loudly are useless exercises that presume authority that may not apply to the problem. Faith is a spiritual essence leading to physical action. It is an action resulting from intelligent understanding. "I know that God will…" is a concrete statement based on previous experience. If you will learn of Him, then you will benefit from His promises. It can be reality, if you will. The question is, "Will you?"

DAY 295

UNSTOPPABLE

"Many are the afflictions of the righteous, but the Lord delivers him out of them all. He guards all his bones; not one of them is broken."
–*Psalm 34:19-20*

Three Things

1. The righteous will face many afflictions
2. The Lord delivers them out of all afflictions
3. He will not allow a bone to be broken

Why should the righteous face afflictions in this world? A faith that is untested is not a faith strengthened. As the Lord was afflicted, why should we find it strange that we also are facing affliction? But be strong and of good courage, beloved. For the Lord will deliver you from such afflictions as He deems fit. Should you fall, He will guard your bones so that none will be broken. Scripture declares that a righteous man may fall seven times, yet he will rise again, which affirms that we can continue. Count it all joy when we are challenged by such adversity. It is just another affliction we survived. We are unstoppable.

LET'S DO IT

"But be doers of the word, and not hearers only, deceiving yourselves." –*James 1:22*

The Word of God is alive and powerful, designed to change the lives of those who hear it. We understand that there is power in the Word of God. Scripture tells us that God honors His word, even above His name. Yet too often the word is heard and not applied. Truth, righteousness, holiness, faith: these words are heard, but not understood. Subsequently they are not applied to the lives of the hearers. The work of the Word is not done until we have done it in our lives. We hear truth – we practice truthfulness. We hear holy – we practice holiness. We hear faith – we practice faithfulness. If we are to mature in righteousness, we must do the work found in His Word. Leaving that Word in the pew when you leave church will not change your life. Pick up the Word. We have work to do. Let's do it!

BELIEVE UNTO RIGHTEOUSNESS

"For what does the Scripture say? 'Abraham believed God, and it was accounted to him for righteousness.' Now to him who works, the wages are not counted as grace but as debt. But to him who does not work but believes on Him who justifies the ungodly, his faith is accounted for righteousness." –*Romans 4:3-5*

You have heard it before, "…by grace you have been saved, and not of works." It is a gift from God, lest any man should boast. Your righteousness is a gift, so bring your nose down. If you must boast, boast about what Christ did for us all on the cross. Let me say it differently for the new Pharisees in training: it is not about you. It is about Jesus. Now that we have that straight, don't stop working on your gifts. They are free to you, but the Lord paid dearly for them. Locate them, strengthen them, and present them to those who need them. Your gifts will make room for you and bring you before great men. Then you can tell them about Jesus. Believe unto righteousness.

DAY 298

A SURE REWARD

"The wicked man does deceptive work, but he who sows righteousness will have a sure reward." – *Proverbs 11:18*

Three Things

1. All work brings a return
2. Wicked men work deception for their reward
3. The righteous sow and reap sure rewards

You cannot trust wicked men who do deceptive work. Their mouths speak one thing, but their hands produce something else. The righteous sow righteousness and they reap a pure reward. Be aware that all work brings some sort of return. If you admire deception and follow wickedness, the return will destroy all that you hold dear. If you are determined to sow righteousness, be aware that the work is impossible. The ground is hard, conditions will challenge you, and people will mock you. But with the guidance of the Holy Spirit, the impossible becomes reality! Work diligently for the sure reward.

A GOOD DAY TO TRUST

"In You, O Lord, I put my trust; let me never be put to shame. Deliver me in Your righteousness, and cause me to escape; incline Your ear to me, and save me." *–Psalm 71:1-2*

Three Things

1. I trust You, Lord. Don't make me ashamed
2. Deliver me with Your righteousness
3. Hear my cry and save me

Trusting the Lord is fundamental for those who believe. We declare our faith to others who need Him, assured that we will not ever be ashamed of our faith. God will help us to escape every snare of the enemy. He will guide us with His eye and light our path, scripture declares. His righteousness will deliver us. Yet, should we be caught fast in dander, He will hear our cry, and save us. What have we to fear, unless we have decided, in disobedience, not to believe in Him. Today is a good day to trust in the Lord. Trust Him now for your salvation.

THE RIGHT PATH

"Do not enter the path of the wicked, and do not walk in the way of evil." –*Proverbs 4:14*

Three Things

1. Paths are known by the people who walk it
2. Avoid the path of the wicked
3. Do not walk in the way of evil

Everybody knows the path, the hall, or the street by which the wicked travel. If you follow the actions of others, you will become like them. The way of evil will only lead to more evil. So why do people venture in that direction? Some are naïve, too innocent to believe that danger exists. Some are prideful, declaring that they are too strong to be swayed by evil. Many are just following the crowd, convinced that popular opinion will prove right. Scripture reminds us that the wide road of such disobedience leads to destruction. Stay on the narrow path of righteousness that leads to heaven. That is the path God chose for you. The Right Path.

NO SHAME HERE

"For I am not ashamed of the gospel of Christ, for it is the power of God to salvation for everyone who believes, for the Jew first and also for the Greek. For in it the righteousness of God is revealed from faith to faith; as it is written, 'The just shall live by faith.'"
–Romans 1:16-17

The gospel of Jesus Christ is precious on every level. It encourages those who are in despair and matures those who believe. When all appears lost, there is the gospel. When joy unspeakable hits our soul, it is because of the love of Jesus. It is the gospel. No discrimination here. The gospel is for whosoever will believe. The gospel reveals the righteousness of God and the plan of God for man to reach righteousness through Jesus Christ. Little faith grows greater faith as we gain knowledge about God's love. We live by faith and learn to be just. We are known for our love and are not ashamed.

DAY 302

LET LOVE CONQUER

"A brother offended is harder to win than a strong city, and contentions are like the bars of a castle." –*Proverbs 18:19*

Three Things

1. Brothers do get offended periodically
2. It is hard to win back their trust
3. Contentions with them are hard

When you offend a brother, one who is close to you and knows you well, he takes it hard. We have seen that in families, where two brothers may not speak to each other for years. It becomes hard to win back the trust of the one offended, and contention becomes bitter and hard. Defenses are always up, and it is like two enemies in battle, rather than two brothers who love each other. Scripture reminds us to forgive abundantly (seventy times seven), and to love excessively (even your enemies). Above all, remember that blood and DNA do not determine who is family. When another has accepted Christ, they are now brothers and sisters in Christ. Love conquers all things, even offenses. Let your love for the Lord conquer and maintain your love for each other.

GOD CAN CARRY IT

"Cast your burden on the Lord, and He shall sustain you; He shall never permit the righteous to be moved." –*Psalm 55:22*

Three Things

1. We all carry burdens
2. Cast your burdens on the Lord, and He shall sustain you
3. He shall never permit the righteous to be moved

Even the righteous deal with the burdens of life. But those who are the children of God can cast their burdens upon Him. Exchange that heavy burden for the light yoke of the Lord. Any challenge He sets before you is designed to strengthen and teach you, not destroy you. When the Lord sets you on assignment to a place, He will sustain you. Also, He will prevent the forces of the enemy from moving you away from your place of assignment. Be aware of the wind of resistance, but never fear them. God can carry it all.

DAY 304

GROW UP

"When I was child, I spoke as a child, I understood as a child, I thought as a child; but when I became a man, I put away childish things." *–1 Corinthians 13:11*

It is easy to allow childish behavior and attitudes to slip into our work as adults. Selfish, entitled, and prideful behaviors can taint the witness of those who refuse to grow up. By faith we accept salvation and through perseverance we push through the painful realities of life. Scripture reveals that we shall not live by bread alone, but by every word that proceeds from the mouth of God. So, we must hear the Word, understand the Word, and do the Word. That is the process of maturing in the Word. We cannot plant a Word of faith that we do not understand. And no one will follow a person who has not walked the road he proclaims. It is time to grow up and gather. The harvest is plentiful. We need mature saints to work in it.

ROOM FOR LOVE

"Therefore they shall eat the fruit of their own way, and be filled to the full with their own fancies." *–Proverbs 1:31*

Three Things

1. We choose what we want
2. We reap the fruit of our own way when we choose that way
3. Being full of your own fancies can be heavy

When people reject the advice of the Lord and choose to go their own way, the result may not satisfy. Bitter fruit grows along the path of sin and disobedience. Those who choose to reap disobedience may find that the taste of it is not desirable. Stubbornly continuing along that way can fill one with anger, bitterness, and disappointment – leaving no room for love, joy, or hope when you are full of your own fancies. Scripture advises us to taste and see that the Lord is good. Just a taste will encourage us to fill our soul with the joy of the Lord. That is a sweet savor to our soul. Always room for more love.

A NEED FOR POWER

"Be exalted, O Lord, in Your own strength! We will sing and praise Your power." *–Psalm 21:13*

Three Things

1. Power and strength are the Lord's
2. He is exalted in His strength
3. We sing and praise His power

To survive, we must have strength. So many will seek and claim the power that can only belong to the Lord. Scripture reminds us that all power is in His hand. He gives us grace to overcome, strength to endure, and power to love. His grace is sufficient for the work. We must strengthen our faith and be content to know that He alone is God. You have all you need to perform the work He sent you to complete. Do not be deceived into desiring to impress anyone with power and strength that you do not possess. When you are weak, then He is strong. Praise Him for His power. It is all you need.

DAY 307

LOOKS LIKE A SHEPHERD

"He can have compassion on those who are ignorant and going astray, since he himself is also subject to weakness. Because of this he is required as for the people, so also for himself, to offer sacrifices for sins. And no man takes this hope to himself, but he who is called by God, just as Aaron was." *–Hebrews 5:2-4*

The job description for Pastors is set clearly in scripture: servant, shepherd, leader. Ignoring the modern corporate requirements that some churches want, the Pastor is called by God to serve God's people. Compassion is crucial as we offer the sacrifice of prayer, minister the Word of God, and seek the Lord for wisdom and guidance. But he is also called to care for the souls of the sheep assigned to his pasture. So, the sheep are to follow the shepherd as the shepherd follows Jesus. Here is some advice: if the church maintains a nurturing and holy environment, the Pastor loves the Lord, and himself provides a healthy diet of God's Word; it might be a good idea to stay there and grow. Wandering sheep become lunch. If he looks like a shepherd, sounds like a shepherd, and lives as a shepherd – He is probably being built by God into a shepherd.

SHINE YOUR LIGHT

"For the commandment is a lamp, and the law a light; reproofs of instruction are the way of life." *–Proverbs 6:23*

Three Things

1. God's commandments light our path
2. Correction helps us live and learn
3. There is only one way of life

God gave us His commandments to guide us away from sin that would destroy us. The light of His law illuminates the path we must walk in this life. If we are not walking in the light of God, we are walking the path of death. Scripture reveals that God disciplines those that He loves. That correction helps us to live in righteousness and to learn holiness. Although some profess to know many paths leading to God, there is only one Way leading to eternal life with God. That Way is through Jesus Christ. He alone is the way, the truth, and the life. Believers, if others around you cannot find that truth, it may be because you have hidden your light. Remove the bushel – let the light of truth shine.

LOOKING FOR MERCY

"Unto You I lift up my eyes, O You who dwell in the heavens. Behold, as the eyes of servants look to the hand of their masters, as the eye of a maid to the hand of her mistress, so our eyes look to the Lord our God, until He has mercy on us." –*Psalm 123:1-2*

Three Things

1. I look to God in heaven for help
2. Some depend on man for support
3. We seek mercy from God

Everyone needs help sometimes. We learn to look to those responsible for our support as we grow. But everything belongs to God. He provides for our needs even through the hands and hearts of man. A mark of spiritual maturity is the ability to trust completely on the Lord. We work with our hands but entrust our heart to Him who first loved us. Scripture reminds us that when we are weak, then is He strong. Can your faith be made complete in such weakness? Turn your eyes to Jesus and let Him show you. Lord, have mercy. We need you.

DAY 310

PRUNING SEASON IS HERE

"As You sent Me into the world, I also have sent them into the world. And for their sakes I sanctify Myself, that they also may be sanctified by the truth." *–John 17:18-19*

As Jesus showed obedience to the Father, we show obedience to Jesus. The model is clear: Jesus was sent into the world and He in turn sends us into that world. God loved the world enough to give His son. As we are saved by grace, through faith, we return to the world to share the light of the gospel. Jesus did not send us into the church, but into the world that needs what the Lord has given to us: the Truth and Love. So many have decided to sit in the sanctuary until Jesus returns, forgetting that the harvest is outside the church and is waiting for willing hearts and working hands. Ask yourself as you sit in your pew, "Am I bearing fruit for the Lord?" If not, know that it is pruning season. Whatever is not bearing fruit for the Lord will be pruned. Selah.

TOO STRONG TO FIGHT

"For as the churning of milk produces butter, and wringing of the nose produces blood, so the forcing of wrath produces strife."
–*Proverbs 30:33*

Three Things

1. One action produces a reaction
2. Some reactions are good, others are not
3. Forcing a fight is not good

For every action, there is an equal and opposite reaction. We know that as a basic law of physics. But such equations exist in the spiritual realm as well. Scripture informs us that we will reap what we sow. In the case stated here, if you force (sow) wrath (anger, discord), you will produce (reap) strife (a fight). An old urban proverb gives advice regarding such instances: "If you don't want trouble, don't start trouble." Avoid violence and don't generate it. We who are Christians are called to walk in peace and love. Our faith makes us powerful, too strong to fight. Humility is an amazing strength.

NO SECRET TO GOD

"If we had forgotten the name of our God, or stretched out our hands to a foreign god, would not God search this out? For He knows the secrets of the heart." *–Psalm 44:20-21*

Three Things

1. If you forget God, or worship idols, God knows
2. He searches out the truth
3. He knows the secrets of the heart

Our outward actions cannot fool God. If we forget God's name while worshipping other gods, He knows. When we stand among worshippers with our hands outstretched and our thoughts preoccupied with money, He knows. When we pray fervently for God to grant favor upon our career or business even while we are cheating customers, He knows. He knows the intentions of our heart. Scripture reveals that we ask and do not receive because we ask amiss, that we may spend it on our pleasures. How does He know? Your heart is no secret to God.

IT IS SIMPLE

"Yet it shall not be so among you; but whoever desires to become great among you shall be your servant. And whoever of you desires to be first shall be slave of all." *–Mark 10:43-44*

There is no competition among the people of God. Questions of who has greater stature and more influence is not settled by church size or attendance. The number of people sitting in the building is not as important as the number trained to go out into the harvest. You may not be able to preach them into obedience, but you can love them into awareness of our purpose on earth. When we cease to pursue more numbers in pews, more dollars in the offering plates, and more square footage in our buildings, then we can focus on strengthening the inner man. When we serve stronger, we love deeper. As we become known more for our love than our preaching, we draw closer to Jesus. Simply teach, simply serve, simply love. Faithfulness is that simple.

LISTEN TO A HOLY TONGUE

"A lying tongue hates those who are crushed by it, and a flattering mouth works ruin." *–Proverbs 26:28*

Three Things

1. Lies and flattery can destroy
2. Lies are intended, showing hatred
3. Flattery deceives, hiding truth

People are always talking, and you may not know the intent of their words until the result manifests. God's words will not return to Him void, because He speaks truth. But Satan is a liar and uses the tongue of others to kill, steal, and to destroy. A lying tongue comes from the Father of Lies (Satan) and shows hatred as it targets the innocent. A flattering tongue is more subtle, seeking to appeal to pride as it targets. Pride always destroys. Walk in righteousness, speak truth, and do not think more highly of yourself than you should. At the end of your journey, a holy tongue will say, "Well done!"

A SECOND OPINION

"The righteous also shall see and fear, and shall laugh at him, saying, 'Here is the man who did not make God his strength, but trusted in the abundance of his riches, and strengthened himself in his wickedness.'" –Psalm 52:6-7

Three Things

1. God destroys, making the righteous laugh
2. Make God your strength
3. Trust not riches or wickedness

Wicked men are judged by God every day, all over the world. The righteous use such men as examples, pointing out their rejection of God, and reliance on their riches or wickedness. This reminds us all to take heed, lest we fall. Somehow the enemy of our soul continues to convince many that rejecting righteousness is a better way to enjoy life. Sin has a terrible price to pay. No one can escape the judgment of God. Is a temporary gain of riches and earthly power worth an eternity in hell? I think not. Ask the man who rejected God what he thinks. Just in case you need a second opinion.

LIFT HIM HIGHER

"Now is the judgment of this world; now the ruler of this world will be cast out. And I, if I am lifted up from the world, will draw all peoples to Myself." *–John 12:31-32*

We are hereby warned. The judgment on this world is now. Could that explain the plagues, wars, lies, and hatred which seems to bloom unabated today? In the midst of them, there is a promise: "If I am lifted up from the world, I will draw all peoples to Myself." We know that Jesus Christ was lifted on the cross to pay for our sins. But is He lifted up from the world today? Has our reverence for the Lord been designated to specific times and places? I get the impression at times that even those who claim the name of Christ have pushed Him down into the dust, rather than lifting Him up. Does your life bring Him glory? Would His face flush with shame at your behavior? It is time to make a change. Lift Him higher.

FRIEND OR FOE

"By pride comes nothing but strife, but with the well advised is wisdom." –*Proverbs 13:10*

Three Things

1. We can learn from many things
2. Pride teaches and brings strife
3. Being well advised brings wisdom

Choose the source of education you prefer, and your life will reveal it. Being prideful brings you into circles of other prideful people, each claiming their own place. Strife will follow. This teaches anger, violence, and hatred. But choose the company of those educated, knowledgeable, and tested in regard to living righteously, and the result is wisdom. Those who seek wisdom will find her and be rewarded with eternal blessings. No need for pride, jealousy, or selfishness. There is enough for all. Scripture reminds us that he who wins souls is wise. Make enemies through strife or make disciples to share the spiritual battle. You choose. Do you want another foe, or a friend you can depend upon?

DO YOU KNOW HIM?

"The Lord preserves all who love Him, but all the wicked He will destroy. My mouth shall speak the praise of the Lord, and all flesh shall bless His holy name forever and ever." –*Psalm 145:20-21*

Three Things

1. The Lord preserves all who love Him, but will destroy the wicked
2. My mouth will praise Him
3. All flesh shall bless His holy name

Do you love the Lord? You will be preserved by Him. All the wicked will be destroyed. No matter what opinion is expressed, all flesh will one day praise His name. Scripture accentuates this fact, "Every knee shall bow, and every tongue confess that Jesus Christ is Lord." I will not wait for that time. I praise His name right now. His praise shall continually be in my mouth. I don't know what He has done for you, but I have every reason to believe and to thank Him. Better step back when I begin to speak the words – "Let me tell you about the Jesus I know." Do you know Him?

CROWN OF TRIALS

"My brethren, count it all joy when you fall into various trials, knowing that the testing of your faith produces patience. But let patience have its perfect work, that you may be perfect, and complete, lacking nothing." –*James 1:2-4*

Trials come and go, leaving behind the truth that God is forming us with each event. Wisdom grows as we see each scar remaining from the winds of adversity. So, we learn to be obedient. We no longer hide from the God-directed storms of life, but triumph in the knowledge that He deems us worthy. Let us learn the difference between trials that God uses to test our faith and the trials that we stumble into because of our own foolishness. Although we learn from truth, it is foolish to boast of disobedience. Endure God's trials, they lead to a crown.

DO SNAKES SMILE?

"Do not eat the bread of a miser, nor desire his delicacies; for as he thinks in his heart so is he. 'Eat and drink!' he says to you, but his heart is not with you." –*Proverbs 23:6-7*

Three Things

1. Do not dine with misers
2. You cannot read another's heart
3. Selfish people do not care about you

Be careful who you fellowship with. Some will possess things that can tempt you to befriend them, but they do not truly want to share. Their smiles and friendly manner can hide true intentions. Scripture warns that the enemy comes to kill, steal, and destroy. When a selfish person is able to take away your peace, they are now working for the enemy. It is better to grow your own grain and make your own bread. In the meantime, tread carefully. Even snakes have been known to smile. Never seen a snake smile? Don't get close enough to find out.

THANK GOD

"Oh, that men would give thanks to the Lord for His goodness, and for His wonderful works to the children of men!" –*Psalm 107:15*

Three Things

1. Men should give thanks to the Lord
2. For His goodness to them
3. And His wonderful works to their children

God blesses in abundance. His goodness covers both men and their children. Prayers for mercy brings wonderful works that bless the children of men. Scripture advises that the fervent prayer of a righteous man avails much. So, we pray when there is a need. We give testimony about the many blessings resulting from God's wonderful works. Consider that your house is more blessed by watching you in prayer to God. They will learn that God honors the obedience in our heart when they see that you demonstrate such obedience. Thank God for all things!

A WORTHY QUESTION

"And He said to them, 'What do you want Me to do for you?'
–Mark 10:36

Far too often we come to the Lord seeking something. He knows what we need even before we ask. Yet He is so gracious. He grants much without expecting anything in return. Consider the irony of that situation. He loved us when we were His enemy, died that we might live, and forgave our sins. Yet His request that we go into the world and make disciples has been forgotten under our worldly "opportunities". His love is to be shared, but we seek only for ourselves. Some have become so selfish that they secretly hate themselves and will hurt others along with themselves. This should not be so. Enter a new season of trust in faith. Ask the Lord, "What do You want me to do for You, Lord? Here am I, send me!" The love He covers you with will be overwhelming and precious. He is worth it, so seek to be worthy.

WISDOM IS THE WAY

"For by me your days will be multiplied, and years of life will be added to you." *–Proverbs 9:11*

Three Things

1. We need the benefits of wisdom
2. It adds days to our existence
3. It increases life for us

One who acquires wisdom will experience longer life and a better enjoyment of the life they live. Wisdom teaches what to believe, what to avoid, what to acquire, what to release, and what path to follow. Scripture advises us to have faith in God, and wisdom helps us to know the God of Truth. Many false prophets stand on mountaintops and in the doorways of large institutions declaring the words they think the world wants to hear. But test the spirits to know if they are of God. Deception abounds in the playgrounds of life. Let wisdom guide you through faith to God, Wisdom knows the Way.

IN THE SANCTUARY

"So I have looked for You in the sanctuary, to see Your power and Your glory." *–Psalm 63:2*

Three Things

1. We seek the Lord in many places
2. We can find Him in the sanctuary
3. We will see His power and glory

We seek God in many places, for scripture notes that if we seek Him, we will find Him. If we look in the Sanctuary where His Spirit dwells, we may also see His power and glory. As His train filled the Temple, so His spirit fills our heart. When two or more are gathered, He is also present. Some can see His power demonstrated in the changed lives of the people that have been touched by the truth of the gospel. We see the glory of the Lord reflected in the love we have, one to another. It has been too long. Let us come into the House of the Lord and worship His presence. No pretending, no comparing. Just the Body of Christ loving Him and each other. He is waiting for us.

DO THE RIGHT WORK

"But you be watchful in all things, endure afflictions, do the work of an evangelist, fulfill your ministry." *–2 Timothy 4:5*

The world is fickle, chasing every new sensation and believing anything that sounds good. Crowds indicate the power of a man and those with money are seen as leaders. But this is not the method by which scripture measures the effectiveness of a ministry. We are to go into all the world (where the truth is needed), not finding programs to fill seats. We are to make disciples, changing lives and building faith, not putting on bigger shows. And we are to show the fruit of our work: stronger families, and deeper roots of faith in God. Not overflowing bank accounts, multiple cars, and mansions for our own family to enjoy. Watch and pray. Consider the work you are doing for the kingdom of God. Will He be pleased with your work? Check your heart, it directs your work for Him. Do the right work.

DAY 326

NO FUN IN SIN

"Who rejoice in doing evil, and delight in the perversity of the wicked." –*Proverbs 2:14*

Three Things

1. People find joy in what they love
2. Some rejoice in doing evil
3. Others delight in the perversity of the wicked

Evil exists in many forms and is accepted by far too many people as just a slight problem. We see the ones who do evil and wonder how they could rejoice in doing the things they do. But there are many more who delight in the perversity of the wicked than those actually engaged in doing evil. Those people have no courage to perform evil acts but admire and support those who do. Scripture reminds us that God sent His Son to condemn sin in the flesh. God is not pleased with sin in any form. If we accept and support evil, are we not expressing what is in our own heart? If we ae to live according to God's Word, we simply must turn away from sin, and avoid those who work iniquity. It may seem like just plain fun, but hell is not an amusement park. When you embrace sin, you are plotting your path to hell. That is not fun.

QUIET WORSHIP

"Truly my soul silently waits for God; from Him comes my salvation." *–Psalm 62:1*

Three Things

1. Good things are worth waiting for
2. My soul waits silently for God
3. He brings my salvation

Some things we celebrate loudly, surrounded by people of like personalities. It is for those things that we have worked hard to achieve and are appreciated by others who care for us. The best things are worth waiting for. The gift of salvation brings a quiet awe to my spirit. How can the God of the Universe love me so? I cannot help but to be silent in the presence of His glory. With man I can declare and shout, but with God I humbly bow, silent before His holiness. His presence strengthens and assures. But His glory requires worship. Even more so when I consider that God waited for me. He patiently stood until I was ready to accept and love Him. I guess I was worth waiting for. So, when I am in the presence of God, hush. Be still and know that He is God. Engage with me in quiet worship.

SERVE THE BODY

"For I have given you an example, that you should do as I have done to you. Most assuredly, I say to you, a servant is not greater than his master; nor is he who is sent greater than he who sent him."
–*John 13:15-16*

Jesus came to seek and to save those who are and were lost; and then He sends us into all the world to spread the gospel and make disciples. He served man and loved the world. How is it that we have come to elevate ourselves and love the wealth of the world? We now seem to use people and love money. This should not be so. We cannot serve two masters. So, if you have decided to let money be your consuming focus, you must repent and serve God instead. If Jesus served, why shouldn't you? Serve others with your gifts, not just the church organization where you attend. The Body of Christ is larger than any organization. You are equipped to serve the Body of Christ, not yourself.

DIFFERENT IS GOOD

"As snow in summer and rain in harvest, so honor is not fitting for a fool." –*Proverbs 26:1*

Three Things

1. There is a proper time for everything
2. Snow in summer, and rain in harvest is wrong
3. Honor is not right for a fool

Wrong weather is confusingly inconvenient. It can damage crops and bring danger to those who are not prepared for it. A fool who receives honor for doing foolish things only encourages more foolishness. It is better to understand the nature of what you face and adjust your response! As for fools, respond to them accordingly. Speaking of proper fit, how do you fit in your place? Do they know that you are a Christian? If your faith speaks confidently, you will stand out when things are not right. Be different. Different is good.

NO OTHER GOD

"You are the God who does wonders; You have declared Your strength among the peoples." –*Psalm 77:14*

Three Things

1. There is only one true God
2. You are the God who does wonders
3. You declare Your strength among people

Many people have worshipped gods of their own making, deceived by evil in their hearts. Only You can do wonders in the world that You created, Lord. You alone can stand and declare Your strength among the peoples. When Your voice is heard, every knee shall bow. None can stand before Your glory. Knowing the truth puts the onus on me to declare it to all that will listen. My heart breaks for those who refuse to see that You alone are God. There is no other.

LIVING ANEW

"Or do you not know that as many of us as were baptized into Christ Jesus were baptized into His death? Therefore we were buried with Him through baptism into death, that just as Christ was raised from the dead by the glory of the Father, even so we also should walk in newness of life." –*Romans 6:3-4*

The old man has passed away, and a new day has arrived. Yet too often, we let doubt and fear keep us buried in the darkness of vain religion. We hide our light under a bushel, passing the burden of ministry onto those with a title – forgetting that you are saints of God, fellow workers, in the harvest. Jesus did not say, "Go ye and get a title." He said to go and make disciples. Let the Holy Spirit refresh the fire that first drew you to faith. Then go share that flame with the world. Walk in newness of life.

DAY 332

TWISTS AND TURNS

"The foolishness of a man twists his way, and his heart frets against the Lord." –*Proverbs 19:3*

Three Things

1. Man has two ways: foolish or wise
2. Foolishness twists his way
3. His heart will then fret against the Lord

If left to devise his own way, man will gravitate toward foolishness. That is the nature already in him. Unfortunately, that very foolishness can twist and confuse his way, leading to regret. The refrain of "I wouda, I couda, I shouda" is taught by those who took the twisted path of foolishness. Even as the Holy Spirit tries desperately to direct his path, the foolish man's heart frets against the Lord. So, he steps away from the path of safety and onto the path of danger in this world. Get off the path of rebellion and foolishness. Hear the wisdom from Him who created the path of righteousness for us. You will avoid the twists and turns that bring confusion. You won't regret it.

PEACE, BE STILL

"He calms the storm, so that its waves are still. Then they are glad because they are quiet; so He guides them to their desired haven."
–Psalm 107:29-30

Three Things

1. God calms the storm and waves
2. We are glad when the waves are quiet
3. He guides us to our desired haven

Turmoil and storms are not good for those seeking to reach safety. Instinctively, in the midst of chaos and opposition, we cry out, lash out, and seek to get out of the danger we are in. We yell for peace (shalom) and seek a place of safety (love and comfort), which is only there when the Lord calms the storms within us. Your words of eternity to come, your attempt to share the gospel, will fall on closed ears until He bids the waves to be still in their lives. Before you launch out into their choppy sea, know that you may not understand the condition of their boat. Send word of His love first, and He will save them. Walk in the peace of His love.

STRONG COMMANDMENTS

"'Teacher, which is the greatest commandment in the law?' Jesus said to him, 'You shall love the Lord your God with all your heart, with all your soul, and with all your mind.' This is the first and great commandment. And the second is like it: 'You shall love your neighbor as yourself.' On these two commandments hang all the Law and the Prophets." *–Matthew 22:36-40*

There is a hint of pride in those who claim to observe Old Testament rules and commandments and claim some promises that do not really belong to them. But if we are to walk in obedience to any commandment, these given by Jesus will lead to peace and profit. Love is the bottom line here. At a time when many seek power, recognition, and financial gain, we should be obvious for our love one to another. Changing the world begins by changing ourselves. And the element for change is Love. Honest, true love. Follow Jesus and obey His strong commandments.

WISE COUNSEL

"The way of a fool is right in his own eyes, but he who heeds counsel is wise." –*Proverbs 12:15*

Three Things

1. We are free to choose life's path for ourselves
2. A fool feels that his ways are always right
3. A wise person heeds good counsel

There are some who refuse advice from those who are wiser. Somehow, the opinions of the crowd draw them toward bad choices. "They say…" is the entryway to suffering in many instances. Yet, "they" are never around to pick you up when their advice leads to your injury or problem. There is no shame in not knowing. When you have decided to be willfully ignorant and reject advice from those wiser than you, there will be shame enough to share. Scripture reminds us to get wisdom. And in getting it, get understanding. That sounds like good advice for us all.

CHOOSE HIS TEACHING

"I have restrained my feet from every evil way, that I may keep Your word. I have not departed from Your judgments, for You Yourself have taught me." *–Psalm 119:101-102*

Three Things

1. I avoid every evil way
2. I have not departed from Your judgments
3. You have taught me

Evil ways are not my path, and I walk rightly to keep Your Word. I do not depart from Your judgements, for in them are the work of righteousness. When I open Your word, You teach me in the way everlasting. Your Holy Spirit opens my understanding that I may know the truth of Your word. Many choices are placed before us daily, so we must restrain ourselves to avoid walking in wrong paths. When we choose rightly, God teaches righteously. When we choose wrongly, we miss God's voice. Choose His teaching.

SECRET REVEALED

"The mystery which has been hidden from ages and from generations, but now has been revealed to His saints. To them God willed to make known what are the riches of the glory of this mystery among the Gentiles: which is Christ in you, the hope of glory."
–*Colossians 1:26-27*

So many spend their lives searching for the meaning of life; the riches of this world. It is not a mystery to be found in the mountains or folded into ancient sage codes. The secret of the mystery is in you: Christ in you, the hope of glory. When you asked Him to dwell in your heart, to be the Lord over your life, He came. He brought amazing gifts and treasures with Him. Yet you do not let the Holy Spirit activate those riches in you. You have not because you ask not. Seek those riches within you for the right reasons, and the secret will be revealed to you and to the world through you.

DAY 338

WHO'S CELEBRATING?

"When the righteous rejoice, there is great glory; but when the wicked arise, men hide themselves." –*Proverbs 28:12*

Three Things

1. Celebrations come from righteous or wicked times
2. Righteous rejoicing brings glory to God
3. Wicked arise to destroy; prudent men hide to avoid such people

What do the people celebrate? Everything. When God brings favor to the righteous, they rejoice with glory to His name. But when God allows the wicked to arise, they celebrate their time of victory. When the wicked arise, know that the enemy will advance his goal to kill, steal, and destroy. When this season comes, wise men hide themselves until the darkness passes. When the roar of celebration is heard, inquire to learn the reason and who is celebrating. Celebrating evil is not wise. Find the cleft of the Rock for safety, then rejoice for His protection.

CRY OF YOUR HEART

"Help us, O God of our salvation, for the glory of Your name; and deliver us, and provide atonement for our sins, for Your names sake."
–Psalm 79:9

Three Things

1. God of our salvation will help us
2. He will deliver us and provide atonement for our sins
3. All for His glory and His name's sake

All that He does for us counts as glory to His name. Salvation, deliverance, atonement for our sins: He does all for His name's sake. Even His love is a sign of His grace. Scripture notes that we love Him because He first loved us. Count it all joy that He freely gives all. So, call out beloved. He waits to hear the sound of your voice. But don't just cry out in need. Cry out in worship and cry out in love. He will respond to the cry of your heart.

WALK IN WORSHIP

"…But we urge you brethren, that you increase more and more; that you also aspire to lead a quiet life, to mind your own business, and to work with your own hands, as we commanded you, that you may walk properly toward those who are outside, and that you may lack nothing." *–1 Thessalonians 4:10b-12*

Christian life is much more than a participation with people in a church building. There is no time or boundary assigned to faith. But sometimes we must remind ourselves and urge others to behave in a way worthy of our position as believers. We are Ambassadors of Christ, citizens of heaven assigned to represent Him while we are on earth. So, we lead lives of quiet faith, busily using our gifts and skills to attract good attention to Him. As we walk properly, we seek to hear the words, "What must I do to be saved?" While we labor to make disciples on earth, one day we will hear the words, "Well done" in heaven. Walk in worship. There is no better way to walk.

BE FILLED WITH GOD

"The backslider in heart will be filled with his own ways, but a good man will be satisfied from above." *–Proverbs 14:14*

Three Things

1. Backsliders separate themselves from God
2. Their selfishness fills their lives
3. God rewards the good from above

Some see the blessings of walking with God and begin the journey joyfully. But sin's temptation can draw them into darkness, and they slide back into their former ways. Before long, backsliders have become entangled with those ways that drew them back. A good man considers the effect of his actions on others. He does not let selfishness draw him away from righteousness. He understands that where he steps, others may follow. So, his heart is filled with faith, that his steps will be sure. When you are anchored in the Lord, there is no backsliding. The Lord makes one rich and adds no sorrow to it. Be filled with God.

PRECEPTS FIRST

"Consider how I love Your precepts; revive me, O Lord, according to Your lovingkindness. The entirety of Your Word is truth, and every one of Your righteous judgements endures forever." –*Psalm 119:159-160*

Three Things

1. I love God's precepts
2. I await revival according to His lovingkindness
3. His Word is truth, and His righteous judgments endure forever

Revival comes when we love God's precepts and yield to His lovingkindness. All of God's words are truth and His righteous judgements endure forever. Why do we pray for revival and then reject His precepts? God judges righteously, not in line with man's opinion, or the deep experiences of emotion. When we return to a position of obedience to God's Word, revival will be here. We won't have to search for it or bring in speakers from out of town. We will be living in the movement toward God which is revival of our faith. With all the things that are happening in this world right now, it could be that the warning signs of God's judgement are here. Think carefully as you consider: Do you love His precepts?

HIGHEST WISDOM

"But the wisdom that is from above is first pure, then peaceable, gentle, willing to yield, full of mercy and good fruits, without partiality and without hypocrisy." *–James 3:17*

God's wisdom, the wisdom that is from above, is the only true wisdom. Available to those who ask for it, this wisdom leads to righteousness, godly character, and unselfish actions. The world honors education. And rightly so, as the lack of education is toxic. Some lift up the drive for knowledge. Scripture notes that the knowledge of the Holy One is understanding, and the fear of the Lord is the beginning of wisdom. Don't be fooled by degrees offered by man or wisdom claimed by educated fools. Without God, knowledge only puffs up and leads to hell. Be wise. Choose wisdom from above and live in it.

DAY 344

SEEK TO ESCAPE

"With her enticing speech she caused him to yield, with her flattering lips she seduced him." –*Proverbs 7:21*

Three Things

1. Temptation comes directly to you
2. Enticing speech breaks down resistance
3. Flattery draws us toward sin

Sin's voice can be soft or confident and compelling. The words used can question, tempt, or even challenge. It is the purpose of the words that should make you stop and evaluate yourself. Sin seeks to calm your mind so that you forget to think, blind your soul so that you cannot see the obvious, and inflame your body to desire what is not right. No matter what temptation reveals itself and regardless of the approach, God does not turn His face away. Scripture assures us that God is faithful. He will provide us with a way of escape, even in the heaviest temptation. So, when you feel yourself weakening, look for the escape door. Then run.

THE DAY AWAITS

"All men shall fear, and shall declare the work of God; for they shall wisely consider His doing: The righteous shall be glad in the Lord, and trust in Him. And all the upright in heart shall glory."
–Psalm 64:9-10

Three Things

1. All men shall declare God's work
2. They will wisely consider His day
3. The righteous and upright will trust and glory in Him

One day every knee shall bow, and every tongue confess that Jesus is Lord. Those who did not know will consider all that He has done. The righteous who have trusted in Him will be glad. The upright in heart shall glory at the fulfillment of God's Word. You want to be there, beloved, and all who have accepted Christ will rejoice. But until that day, we have work to do. Share the gospel, live in the truth. Press onward to higher callings. The Day awaits.

YOU ARE ENOUGH

"Let no one despise your youth, but be an example to the believers in word, in conduct, in love, in spirit, in faith, in purity. Till I come, give attention to reading, to exhortation, to doctrine." *–1 Timothy 4:12-13*

According to the world, we will always be too young to do what God has called us to do. Not enough experience, education, political influence, social impact, money, etc. You name it. If you measure your preparation to serve God by the imposed limitations of man's opinions, you will never be good enough. So, step out of the evaluation line. Spend your time walking as a model of a child of God. Read the word and allow the Holy Spirit to build your faith and guide your conduct. Encourage others to accept the gospel and teach them the Way of righteousness. You don't have to prove yourself to those who only seek to find fault. Walk in love. Even they will follow.

TRUE BEAUTY

"Charm is deceitful and beauty is passing, but a woman who fears the Lord, she shall be praised." –*Proverbs 31:30*

Three Things

1. Charm can be learned and may be deceitful
2. Beauty will deteriorate with age and exposure
3. Fear of the Lord is always beautiful

Many chase the attention and rewards that physical beauty brings. We spend money that we do not have to maintain youth and physical attractiveness that cannot be preserved by us. Too often we find that the charm that first drew us and the beauty that captivated us was a mask that hid an evil soul. Pain that comes from contact with spiritual toxicity makes it hard to love others afterwards. Seek to be in the presence of one who loves the Lord. True beauty shines from the heart of those who carry the Holy Spirit within. Any other love is counterfeit. Praise the true beauty of those who seek and love the Lord. That is true beauty.

SING PRAISES

"But I will sing of Your power; yes, I will sing aloud of Your mercy in the morning; for You have been my defense and refuge in the day of my trouble." –*Psalm 59:16*

Three Things

1. Sing of the Lord's power
2. Sing aloud od His mercy
3. He is your defense and refuge

When your heart is full – sing! To tell the world about the power and mercy of the Lord – sing louder! When trouble threatens to overcome you, has He not covered you under His wings? Does not the enemy flee at the mention of His name? In the midst of the storm, His whispered command stills the wind and calms the sea. Of whom shall I be afraid when He walks with me? He alone has made me righteous. So, I will sing of the Lord my God. Sing praises.

CONTENT WITH GOD

"Now godliness with contentment is great gain. For we brought nothing into this world, and it is certain we can carry nothing out. And having food and clothing, with these we shall be content."
–1 Timothy 6:6-8

Some assume that godliness is a means to gain wealth in this world. So, they possess a form of godliness but seek the power of money. Yet even as they heap money to themselves, they are not satisfied. Scripture reminds us to seek first the kingdom of God and His righteousness, and all the things you desire will be added to you. So having true godliness and being content with what God has already provided is great gain. The wealth of the world cannot be taken with us, so we should be content with what we need to live. Heaven does not need our money but the Lord needs our heart so He can bless others with our gifts while we are on the earth. Contentment goes a long way toward appreciating God. It also keeps our mind focused on the work that we have been assigned to complete.

WORTH THE CLIMB

"Wisdom is too lofty for a fool; he does not open his mouth in the gate." –*Proverbs 24:7*

Three Things

1. Wisdom is not for everyone
2. The unknowledgeable will not attain lofty goals
3. He will not enter the discussion leading to more knowledge

Wisdom is not a desired goal for everyone. Some would rather not know than to labor to attain knowledge or wisdom. Willfully ignorant people see wisdom as too lofty to consider. They don't even enter conversations that require strong knowledge or that which will add more to their understanding. Such a condition can be lethal. Especially if the wisdom relates to the area of eternal life. Scripture informs us that the knowledge of God is the beginning of wisdom. That wisdom is definitely worth the climb.

PROTECT THE FOUNDATIONS

"If the foundations are destroyed, what can the righteous do?"
–*Psalm 11:3*

Three Things

1. Foundations are needed for any structure
2. Foundations can be destroyed
3. The righteous need foundations too

Everything is built upon a foundation. Without a foundation, structures will fall. The heaven and earth were created by God's sord: "Let there be…" The body of Christ stands on faith, and obedience to the word of God. When we lose faith that the gospel is true and refuse to obey the Word of God, we are just another social club. We cannot share a gospel we do not believe. And if we reject the fact that the word of God is alive and powerful, those truths will lose its effect for us. What can the righteous do? Stay strong in the faith, obey the word, and protect the foundations provided in the Scripture.

FAILING EACH OTHER

"So then each of us shall give account of himself to God. Therefore let us not judge one another anymore, but rather resolve this, not to put a stumbling block or a cause to fall in our brother's way."
–*Romans 14:12-13*

Ministry is not a competition or a secular business in which we use any means available to add customers to the pews. The enemy works hard to damage the witness of believers. The body of Christ must not add to that conflict. Judging the style of other churches, looking down on the ministry of others, and speaking badly about other Servants of God helps the enemy. When you feel jealousy toward another church; pray for them. When their style of worship offends you; pray for yourself. When a brother or sister in Christ falls into sin; pray for the entire body of Christ. When someone from our own ranks falls, we have failed each other.

THE ULTIMATE FRIEND

"A friend loves at all times, and a brother is born for adversity."
–*Proverbs 17:17*

Three Things

1. Friends are rare and precious
2. Friends love at all times
3. Brothers are born for adversity

True friends are rare in life and are precious to our existence. They share our secrets, help in time of need, and stay in our heart even when far away. A brother is born for adversity, and shared blood brings deeper connection. If we share the blood of Christ with a friend, they can also become our brother. As such, they can be depended upon in the midst of any battle. Scripture reminds us that there is a friend who sticks closer than a brother. Only through the Holy Spirit in us can we learn the truth of that scripture. Seek the companionship of friends and maintain the love of your brother. But never release the closeness of the Holy Spirit. He is the ultimate Friend.

MIRACLE WORKER

"The Lord opens the eyes of the blind; the Lord raises those who are bowed down; the Lord loves the righteous." –*Psalm 146:8*

Three Things

1. The Lord opens eyes that have been blinded
2. He removes burdens of sin that are too heavy to carry
3. He loves the righteous

The Lord removes obstacles that stand between Him and His children. He opens the eyes of those blinded with sin, hatred, and selfishness. He removes the burdens of those under the weight of shame, ignorance, and deception. He lifts us toward righteousness, making our paths straight. When you see someone who was blind and crippled, yet now enters life filled with joy, know that it was the Lord who did the work! Let Him work on your pain. You will thank Him later, for He alone can work miracles!

CAN YOU HEAR HIM?

"But they have not all obeyed the gospel. For Isaiah says, "Lord, who has believed our report?" So then faith comes by hearing, and hearing by the Word of God." –*Romans 10:16-17*

The gospel has gone out to unbelieving ears. The word has not changed, but those receiving it are hampered by distrust and unbelief. "Preach, Pastor!", they declare. But when the sermon ends, they return to a life of doubt. Do they realize that you must hear the gospel to learn of faith, and then live the gospel to strengthen that faith? We must be doers and not just hearers if we are to mature in our service to the Lord. But that is not you, beloved. You hear the truth and let your faith in the truth guide your steps – not seeking miracles but seeking to be a miracle in the life of someone else. As you have risen from the dead in trespasses and sin, you can now hear audibly the voice of God. You are guided by the Holy Spirit and determined to use your gifts to advance the kingdom of God where you are. So, you have learned to listen intently. He is speaking. Can you hear Him?

CONSIDER THE POOR

"The righteous considers the cause of the poor, but the wicked does not understand such knowledge." –*Proverbs 29:7*

Three Things

1. Poverty has a cause
2. The righteous seeks the reason for the poverty
3. The wicked does not care to understand

Everything has a cause. Being poor starts with lack, which is compounded by the responses to that lack. The righteous seeks to find the reason, so He may help. The wicked does not understand the cause and does not care. One who is without Christ will find himself without hope. Having faith leading to Christ results in a hope that cannot be taken away. With that hope, you will never be poor, regardless of the condition of your bank account. The Lord makes rich and adds no sorrow to it. Consider the poor and avoid the cause that leads to poverty.

OPEN THE GATES

"Open to me the gates of righteousness; I will go through them, and I will praise the Lord. This is the gate of the Lord, through which the righteous shall enter." –*Psalm 118:19-20*

Three Things

1. Open the gates of righteousness
2. I will praise the Lord as I go through them
3. Righteous enter through the Lord's gate

We enter the gates of righteous when the Lord opens them. I will enter these gates with praise and thanksgiving, knowing that only the righteous may enter. The Lord has made me righteous as I walk the narrow road of righteousness. I have shared the gospel of love along the Way, so others have chosen to follow. Have you heard? Jesus is the only Way. He alone can open these gates, and welcome His servants with the words, "Well Done!" We are going home soon. Open gates await us.

GO DEEP

"Then He got into one of the boats, which was Simon's, and asked him to put out a little from the land. And He sat down and taught the multitudes from the boat. When He had stopped speaking, He said to Simon, 'Launch out into the deep and let down your nets for a catch.'" –*Luke 5:3-4*

Simon had been fishing in deep water before, but the message was clear. First, we need to launch away from the multitudes, and second, we need Jesus in the boat with us to catch the best fish. When I consider the word "deep", it is not just the physical manifestation that distinguishes the concept. We need to seek deep levels of faith, deeper levels of love, and the deepest levels of sacrifice. A shallow study of the Word will not yield deep understanding, and a shallow application of faith will not yield a greater demonstration of work for God. If you truly want to serve the Lord – go deep. Make sure He is in the boat with you. If you are doing this for yourself, you might as well stay on the shore.

LISTEN CAREFULLY

"Incline your ear and hear the words of the wise, and apply your heart to my knowledge." *–Proverbs 22:17*

Three Things

1. The source of learning matters
2. Listen to the words of the wise
3. Take God's knowledge to heart

Everyone has a voice and an opinion, but we must not listen to words indiscriminately. Lean in to hear the words of those who are wise. Wisdom is granted to those who seek knowledge from the Lord. So, take that knowledge, God's knowledge, and apply your heart to it. Use that knowledge to strengthen your faith and to guide your steps. Let God's word, which is ripe with knowledge, be a lamp to keep your feet from stumbling. As the world increases the volume of words of foolishness, focus on the still quiet voice that leads to peace and righteousness. Incline your ear to the truth. Thy word is Truth.

DAY 360

LOVE IN BATTLE

"For You have armed me with strength for the battle; You have subdued under me those who rose up against me." *–Psalm 18:39*

Three Things

1. God strengthens and subdues
2. We are armed with strength for battle
3. God subdues our enemies

The battle is not ours, it is the Lord's, scripture notes. Yet He arms us with strength to fight the battle. Life and adversity trains us to prepare for battle. But God even subdues our enemies so that they come under our authority. If we are children of God who have come under the authority of Jesus Christ, accepting His gift of salvation, then our victories bring glory to God. Examine your heart, O warrior of God. Do you fight as a representative of God or for yourself? Check your weapons to determine which applies. If there is no love in your arsenal, you might be a rogue warrior, fighting for your own reputation and glory. Love is the most effective weapon when we battle for the souls of men.

WHAT'S NEXT?

"For I have given to them the words which You have given Me; and they have received them, and have known surely that I came forth from You; and they have believed that You sent Me." *–John 17:8*

You have heard the words, read the words, and studied the words. You have received the words, and truly believe that Jesus Christ is Lord. What is next? Now you pray for miracles and revival and are concerned that you do not see them in your presence. The miracle is you. Salvation has delivered you from death. Your life now belongs to the Lord, and revival will come through you when it is evident in you. Seek first the kingdom of God, and all the rest will be added to you. So, the next step for you is not to prove you are a miracle or to try to work a miracle on someone else, but to live in obedience to God's Word. The world you live in will notice the difference and seek to know why - then you can be part of the next miracle. Tell them about Jesus, so they can live again.

YOUR QUIET PRAYER

"The Lord is far from the wicked, but He hears the prayer of the righteous." –*Proverbs 15:29*

Three Things

1. The Lord is far from the wicked
2. He will not allow sin in His presence
3. He hears the prayer of the righteous

The wicked have chosen to live a life that is not pleasing to God, which keeps them distant from Him. Sin is an abomination to the Lord. So, when the wicked have fallen into trouble, they will cry out to the Lord, hoping that He will hear their cries. But they have to cry loudly, as they have distanced themselves from the Lord. But the righteous walk next to the Lord, seeking His will, and honoring His Way. So even their quiet prayers are heard by Him. Scripture reminds us that God inclines His ear to us. Seeking righteousness leads us in the path of righteousness for His name's sake. Our faith pleases Him, and He responds by answering our prayers. No need to cry out, beloved. He hears your prayer. Even the ones that you whisper.

GRACED WITH GRAY

"O God, You have taught me from my youth; and to this day I declare Your wondrous works. Now also when I am old and gray-headed, O God, do not forsake me, until I declare Your strength to this generation, your power to everyone who is to come." *–Psalm 71:17-18*

Three Things

1. You have taught me to declare Your works
2. Now that I am old, do not forsake me
3. I must speak to this generation to declare Your strength

Spreading the gospel is a lifelong venture. God teaches us from our youth and strengthens us to declare His wondrous works. Old age brings wisdom, but we need the strength of the Lord to reach younger generations. We need to have the Spirit of Caleb if we are to conquer the next mountain. The Lord will renew your strength if you do not grow weary in well-doing. If you are blessed to have a gray head, rejoice. Righteousness exalts a nation. Be part of the movement.

DAY 364

PUSH FOR YOUR PURPOSE

"Now My soul is troubled, and what shall I say? 'Father, save Me from this hour?' But for this purpose I came to this hour." –*John 12:27*

Here we are about to step into another year. We have been blessed in many ways, and our work on earth is not yet done. Maybe your soul is troubled by things you failed to finish last year, and you are not sure the direction you should go for the year to come. Let me propose that you consider the statement of Jesus. It reveals that despite uncertainty about the conditions He faced, He knew His purpose. If we let conditions rule our decisions, we may miss our purpose. So, before you rush off to the next chore or project, sit down with your Father and discover your purpose. Study the road to reach your purpose, and then determine to let nothing stop you from reaching it. Everything costs. Pay the price for understanding your purpose. By the way, you do not have to share with everyone what your purpose is. They can see the results when you finish. Push for your purpose.

WISDOM OF PRAYER

"Do not go hastily to court; for what will you do in the end, when your neighbor has put you to shame? Debate your case with your neighbor, and do not disclose the secret to another." *–Proverbs 25:8-9*

Three Things

1. Lawsuits should be done carefully
2. Be certain that you are in the right
3. Keep the issue out of the public

Christians are called to a higher standard regarding legal matters. Lawsuits should be entered into carefully, being certain that their complaint is justified. Scripture reminds us that we are to examine ourselves to see if we are in the faith. If indeed we are guided by love, the element of forgiveness will remove anger and retribution from our relationship with each other. God's law rules over the body of Christ, guiding us to a deeper love for each other. When there is a dispute, don't sue – seek God in prayer. There is wisdom in doing so.

IN CLOSING

Ministry of the Word is an ongoing process. As the world changes, we must find different and more effective ways to serve the word of God to those who need more of Jesus. As a man of God who has discovered that God trains us for each assignment we are to complete, I adjust to the environment that confronts me. In some ways, I take a military approach to each challenge. I will complete the work, regardless of the enemy's attempts to stop the progress.

      Each page of this work is a seed that, if allowed, will encourage the growth of the fruit of the Spirit within you. I remind you to bring your brain with you as you consider the truth and wisdom of each devotional reflection. Ponder the message. Pray for understanding. Should the message of that day not motivate you to seek the Lord further, move on. You might find that it will hit your spirit later. Keep living. The word of God is living and powerful, and sharper than any two-edged sword. It will penetrate.

Author

Pastor Dr. James R. Boyd

Other works by
Author Pastor Dr. James R. Boyd

"Special Forces Christians: The Rise of Militant Faith"

Made in the USA
Columbia, SC
16 August 2024

c33737fc-537c-477e-8eaa-9aea40a46ebdR01